PROMOTION- SERVICE MATTER- SUPREME COURT'S LATEST LEADING CASE LAWS

CASE NOTES- FACTS- FINDINGS OF APEX COURT JUDGES & CITATIONS

JAYPRAKASH BANSILAL SOMANI

ISBN 979-888569167-3

Dedicated

To

All the Past & Present Judges of the Supreme Court of India.

Salute to their wisdom.

Salute to their interpretation of Law.

Salute to their elaborative judgement writing.

Contents

Preface vii

Acknowledgements ix

1. The State Of Kerala And Ors. Vs. Leesamma Joseph, 2021 1
2. Tek Chand And Ors. Vs. Bhakra Beas Management Board And Ors., 2021 3
3. Council Of Architecture Vs. Mukesh Goyal And Ors., 2020 5
4. D. Raghu And Ors. Vs. R. Basaveswarudu And Ors., 2021 9
5. State Of U.p. And Ors. Vs. Vikash Kumar Singh And Ors.,2021 12
6. Union Of India (uoi) And Ors. Vs. N. Murugesan And Ors.,2021 14
7. Mukesh Kumar And Ors. Vs. The State Of Uttarakhand And Ors., 2020 17
8. Registrar Karnataka University And Ors. Vs. Prabhugouda And Ors., 2020 22
9. Union Public Service Commission Vs. Jawahar Santhkumar And Ors., 2019 26
10. Girish Kumar Vs. State Of Maharashtra And Ors., 2019 29
11. Jarnail Singh And Ors. Vs. Lachhmi Narain Gupta And Ors., 2018 33
12. Nawal Kishore Mishra And Ors. Vs. High Court Of Judicature At Allahabad And Ors., 2015 36
13. Hc Pradeep Kumar Rai And Ors. Vs. Dinesh Kumar Pandey And Ors., 2015 40
14. Panchraj Tiwari Vs. M.p. State Electricity Board And Ors., 2014 44
15. Manoj Manu And Ors. Vs. Union Of India (uoi) And Ors., 2013 47
16. State Of Rajasthan Vs. Ucchab Lal Chhanwal, 2013 50
17. Debabrata Dash And Ors. Vs. Jatindra Prasad Das And Ors., 2013 53
18. Tamil Nadu Rural Development Engineers Association Vs. The Secretary To Government Rural Development Department And Ors., 2013 56

Contents

19. Chairman, Rushikulya Gramya Bank Vs. Bisawamber Patro And Ors., 2013 60
20. Union Of India (uoi) And Ors. Vs. Hemraj Singh Chauhan And Ors., 2010 62
21. State Of Uttaranchal And Ors. Vs. Dinesh Kumar Sharma, 2006 66

Videos & Tv Shows On Law & Exim 69

List Of Adv. Jayprakash Somani's Books 75

Preface

Dear Learned Advocates of the Trial Courts, Tribunals, Appellate Tribunals, High Courts, Supreme Court, HR Professionals, Corporates, Govt Recruitment Officers & Employees,

I am very delighted to provide you a book on 'Promotion- Service Matter - Supreme Court of India's Latest Leading Case Laws'.

In this book you will get...

1. Name of the Case i. e. Cause title

2.Relevant Sections discussed in the case

3.Hon'ble Judges/Coram of the case

4.Number of PDF Pages in Original Judgement of the case

5. All available Citations of the case

6. Case Note with appeal allowed/ dismissed or disposed off

7. Facts of the case

8.Hon'ble Apex Court's findings, while dismissing/allowing or disposing the appeal

9. Ratio Decidendi if any.

My special thanks to Manupatra, because of their web portal I can compile this book in well manner. I am also thankful to Notion Press to support me to publish & market this book throughout the Country. Thanks to my Juniors, Advocate Colleagues & Insolvency Professional Colleagues to support me in this venture.

Miss Devpriya Shah has helped me a lot to compile this book.

I hope this book will add some value addition in the wealth of your legal knowledge. Your positive feedbacks will boost me to compile/ write further books & negative feedbacks will improve my skills. Kindly send your valuable feedbacks by email.

Thanks with Regards,

Jayprakash B. Somani

Advocate, Supreme Court of India

Email: jaysomani64@gmail.com

Web Site:www.jayprakashsomani.com

Call: 8384051134, 9322188701, 9318381287

Acknowledgements

Printed & Published by

Notion Press

No. 8, 3rd Cross Street,
CIT Colony, Mylapore,
Chennai, Tamil Nadu- 600004

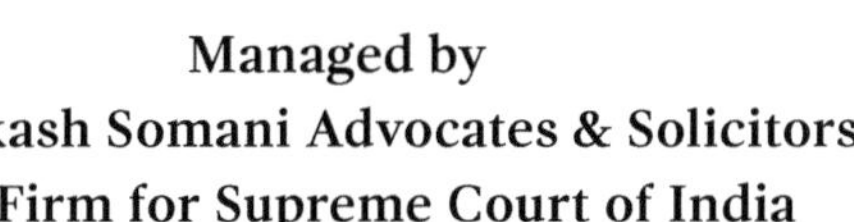

Managed by

Jayprakash Somani Advocates & Solicitors

Law Firm for Supreme Court of India

Delhi Office

257 C, Pocket 1, Mayur Vihar Phase 1, Delhi 110091.
Call 8384051134, 9322188701, 8459194576, 01141051516

Supreme Court Chamber

312, 3rd Floor, M. C. Setalvad Block, In front of 'D' Gate, Bhagwan Das Road, Supreme Court of India, New Delhi 110001
Contact: 8459194576, 9811011747

www.jayprakashsomani.com

Books are available online at

1. **Notion Press:** https://notionpress.com/author/jayprakash_somani
2. **Amazon:** https://www.amazon.in/s?k=jayprakash+somani
3. **Flipkart:** https://www.flipkart.com/search?q=Jayprakash%20Somani

CHAPTER ONE

THE STATE OF KERALA AND ORS. VS. LEESAMMA JOSEPH, 2021

Hon'ble Judges/Coram:

Sanjay Kishan Kaul and R. Subhash Reddy, JJ.

Equivalent Citation: AIR2021SC3076, 2021(5)ALD42, 2021(4)ALT122, 2021 3 AWC2858SC, 2021(4)BLJ280, 2021 (3) CCC 253 , 2021(II)CLR695, 2021(2)ESC594(SC), [2021(170)FLR696], ILR2021(3)Kerala1003, 2021(3)J.L.J.R.66, 2021(3)JLJ137, 2021 (4) KHC 318, 2021(4)KLT191, 2021LabIC3105, 2021(6)MhLj1, (2021)5MLJ196, 2021(4)MPLJ325, 2021(3)PLJR58, (2021)9SCC208, 2021(3)SCT189(SC), 2021(5)SLR811(SC), MANU/SC/0385/2021

Relevant sections: Section 33 of the Persons with Disabilities (Equal Opportunities, Protection of Rights and Full Participation) Act, 1995; The Rights of Persons with Disabilities Act, 2016

Number of pages in original Judgment: 10

Case Note:

Service - Promotion - Rights and equal opportunities - Persons with special abilities (PWD) - The Persons with Disabilities (Equal Opportunities, Protection of Rights and Full Participation) Act, 1995 (1995 Act) - The Rights of Persons with Disabilities Act, 2016 (2016 Act) that replaced the 1995 Act - Impugned order decided in favour of Respondent on her right of promotion under the 1995 Act - Whether the 1995 Act mandates reservations in promotions for persons with disabilities? - Whether reservation under Section 33 of the 1995 Act is dependent upon identification of posts as stipulated by Section 32?

Brief Facts:

Respondent was appointed on compassionate grounds, after her brother had passed away during service. She undisputedly suffered from Post Polio Residual Paralysis (L) Lower Limb and her permanent disability was assessed at 55%. The Respondent subsequently cleared all departmental tests for promotion, and was given due promotions. The issue raised by the Respondent was pertaining to her entitlement to promotions with all consequential benefits under the 1995 Act as she suffered from physical disability. Tribunal dismissed the application seeking relief sought. High Court set aside order of the Tribunal. Hence, the present appeal.

Held, while dismissing the Appeals:

i. What is required is identification of posts in every establishment until exempted under proviso to Section 33. No doubt the identification of the posts was a prerequisite to appointment, but then the appointment cannot be frustrated by refusing to comply with the prerequisite.
ii. The 1995 Act does not make a distinction between a person who may have entered service on account of disability and a person who may have acquired disability after having entered the service. Similarly, the same position would be with the person who may have entered service on a claim of a compassionate appointment. The mode of entry in service cannot be a ground to make out a case of discriminatory promotion.
iii. The course of action followed by the High Court in the impugned order is salutary and does not call for any interference. In fact, what seems to emerge is that the Appellant-State has not implemented the judgment of this Court in Rajeev Kumar Gupta's and Siddaraju's cases. Thus, directions issued to the State of Kerala to implement these judgments and provide for reservation in promotion in all posts after identifying said posts. This exercise should be completed within a period of three months. The appeal is accordingly dismissed in terms aforesaid.

CHAPTER TWO

Tek Chand and Ors. Vs. Bhakra Beas Management Board and Ors., 2021

Hon'ble Judges/Coram:

Navin Sinha and R. Subhash Reddy, JJ.

Equivalent Citation: 2021(9)ADJ701, 2021 4 AWC3161SC, 2021(5)BLJ76, 2021(III)CLR292, 2021(3)ESC705(SC), [2021(171)FLR41], 2021(3)SCT530(SC), 2021(3)SLJ60(SC), MANU/SC/0488/2021

Relevant Section/provisions: Bhakra Beas Management Board Class-III and Class-IV Employees (Recruitment and Conditions of Service) Regulations, 1994 (Regulations)

Number of Pages in the Original Judgment: 06

Case Note:

Service - Promotion - Annulment thereof on the ground of eligibility - Validity - Bhakra Beas Management Board Class-III and Class-IV Employees (Recruitment and Conditions of Service) Regulations, 1994 (Regulations) - High Court directed annulment despite not being prayed for in Petition - Whether High Court travelled beyond its jurisdiction? - Whether Appellant eligible to be considered for promotion?

Brief Facts:

The Appellants were promoted to the post of Leading Fireman under the applicable Regulations. Their promotions however annulled by the High

Court, holding them to be ineligible for promotion under the Regulations. Appellants, submitted to be admittedly senior to R3. Regulation 5 provided that promotion was to be based on the seniority-cum-merit principle. The Appellants held good service record. The Departmental Promotion Committee considered their candidature and promoted them. R3 though did not seek relief for annulling the promotion of Appellants, yet the High Court travelled beyond the pleadings to grant a relief not otherwise sought by R3.

Held, while allowing the Appeals:

i. View taken by the High Court that it was only if a candidate possessed an appreciable initiative and also obtained good reports, then only he was eligible to be considered for promotion, not sustainable. The use of the word 'and' does not make it compulsory for the candidate to possess both because in that event the question of selection from amongst the eligible post on the seniority-cum-merit principle would not apply strictosenso.

ii. Respondent No. 3 had not sought any relief for setting aside the promotion of the Appellants. The High Court travelled beyond the pleadings in annulling the promotion of the Appellants. High Court completely lost sight of the objection of the management that there were many others senior to Respondent No. 3 in the category of Fireman. Appeal allowed holding that the Appellants were eligible to be considered for promotion.

CHAPTER THREE

Council of Architecture Vs. Mukesh Goyal and Ors., 2020

Hon'ble Judges/Coram:

Dr. D.Y. Chandrachud and Ajay Rastogi, JJ.

Equivalent Citation: AIR2020SC1736, 2020(5)BLJ207, 2021(2)BomCR148, 2020(6)MhLj22, (2020)3MLJ645, 2020(4)MPLJ612, 2020(2)RCR(Civil)295, (2020)16SCC446, 2020 (5) SCJ 125, MANU/SC/0305/2020

Relevant sections: Section 37 of Architects Act 1972

Number of pages in original Judgment: 19

Case Note:

Service - Promotion - Practice of architecture - Section 37 of Architects Act 1972 - First Respondent had been working as Architectural cum Planning Assistant in service of Third Respondent-Development Authority and claims to possess degree in architecture - Third Respondent framed Service Regulations for recruitment and promotion of employees in its various departments in which one of departments was Department of Planning and Architecture - Meeting was held by third Respondent to decide whether degree in Architecture and Town Planning and degree in Architecture was necessary for promotion to posts of Associate Town Planner and Associate Architect - Opinion was sought from state government - During this period, promotions to post of Associate Town

Planner and Associate Architect had continued to remain in abeyance, resulting in situation employees being denied consideration for promotion - First Respondent filed writ petitions before High Court - High Court held that Section 37 of Act did not create bar on individuals not registered with Council from carrying out duties and functions of Architect - Hence, present appeal - Whether Section 37 of Architects Act prohibit individuals not registered as architects from practicing activities undertaken by architects and post titled Architect or any other similar title could be held by person not registered as architect under Architects Act.

Brief Facts:

The first Respondent has been working as an Architectural cum Planning Assistant in the service of the third Respondent, Development Authority and claims to possess a degree in architecture from the Indian Institute of Architects. The Development Authority framed the Service Regulations for the recruitment and promotion of employees in its various departments. One of the departments was the Department of Planning and Architecture where the first Respondent is employed. A meeting was held by Development Authority to decide whether a degree in Architecture and Town Planning and a degree in Architecture was necessary for candidates who were to be promoted to the posts of Associate Town Planner and Associate Architect. An opinion was sought from the Mukhya Nagar Gram Niyojak (Town and Country Planning Department). In a letter, the Mukhya Nagar Gram Niyojak recommended that a degree or diploma in the relevant subjects should be an essential qualification for candidates seeking promotion. Development Authority subsequently sought the opinion of the state government on the same question. During this period, promotions to the post of Associate Town Planner and Associate Architect had continued to remain in abeyance, resulting in a situation where employees who have served for as many as twenty-five years being denied consideration for promotion. Before the High Court, the first Respondent filed writ petitions. The High Court held that Section 37 of the Architects Act did not create a bar on individuals not registered with the Council from carrying out the duties and functions of an Architect. The High Court held that Section 37 only prohibits unregistered individuals from using the title architect. In disposing of the writ petitions, the High Court held that the mere nomenclature of the particular post will not in any way be said to violate the provisions of the Architects Act 1971. Therefore, the High Court permitted Development Authority to continue referring to the Class II posts as

Associate Town Planner and Associate Architect.

Held, while partly allowing the appeal:

i. Architecture undoubtedly constitutes a highly specialised profession requiring the possession of minimum educational qualifications. However, architects were by and large engaged by means of a contract for services. In other words, architects provide a set of specialised services towards the larger goal of construction. Architects were not embarking on construction independently of other actors. By virtue of the Architects Act, anybody engaging the services of an individual calling themselves an Architect was assured that such an individual possesses statutorily recognised educational qualifications and is competent to complete the task at hand. It was in this manner that the legislature protects the common person from untrained individuals.

ii. Therefore, it was held that Section 37 of the Architects Act did not prohibit individuals not registered under the Architects Act from undertaking the practice of architecture and its cognate activities.

iii. While this court had held that Section 37 did not prohibit the practice of architecture by unregistered individuals, it certainly does prohibit unregistered individuals from using the title and style of architect. Under the scheme of the Architects Act, only individuals possessing the statutorily recognised minimum educational qualifications can apply for registration as an Architect under the Act. Registration as an architect under the statute was thus a guarantee of possessing certain minimum educational qualifications. Section 37 prohibits unregistered individuals from designating themselves or referring to themselves as architects. The consequence of this regulatory regime was that when an individual was called an Architect a reasonable person would assume that they were a registered architect under the Architects Act and as a consequence possess the requisite educational qualifications and specialised knowledge associated with architects.

iv. In the present case, this court recognise the power of Development Authority to provide and modify the minimum eligibility criteria for promotion of candidates to the posts of Associate Town Planner and Associate Architect. This court further recognise that the authority had significant discretion in how it chooses to title the various posts under its supervision. However, to permit third Respondent to continue to title a post that includes individuals who were not registered architects under the Architects Act as Associate Architect would result in a violation of Section 37 of the Architects Act. In the case of Tulya Gogoi the High Court expressly held that the prohibition on the use of title and style of architect contained in Section 37 of the Architects Act applies to both private individuals and government employees.

CHAPTER FOUR

D. Raghu and Ors. Vs. R. Basaveswarudu and Ors., 2021

Hon'ble Judges/Coram:

Sanjay Kishan Kaul and K.M. Joseph, JJ.

Equivalent Citation: MANU/SC/0125/2020

Relevant sections:

Number of Pages in the Original Judgment: 46

Case Note:

Service - Promotion - Appellants were originally recruited as Data Entry Operators (DEOs) Grade A and had been working as Data Entry Operators Grade B - Appellants, before Tribunal, had called in question legality of notice seeking to confine promotion to post of Inspector, to category of Tax Assistant, Upper Division (UD) Clerk, Stenographer Grade-II, etc. - Tribunal directed Appellants to be considered for promotion to post of Inspectors - Writ Petitions filed against order of Tribunal before High Court - High Court that Appellants were having legal right, under erstwhile Rules, to be considered for promotion to vacancies which arose prior to Rules in regard to post of Inspector - Hence, present appeal - Whether impugned order pertaining to promotion to post of Inspector of Central Excise was sustainable.

Facts:

The Appellants were originally recruited as Data Entry Operators (DEOs) Grade A and had been working as Data Entry Operators Grade B. The Appellants, had called in question the legality of Notice seeking to confine the promotion to the post of Inspector, to category of Tax Assistant,

Upper Division (UD) Clerk, Stenographer Grade-II, etc., with certain years of experience, for promotion. The Tribunal directed the Appellants to be considered for promotion to the post of Inspectors. Writ Petitions came to be filed in High Court against order of the Tribunal. The High Court found that Appellants were having a legal right, under the erstwhile Rules, to be considered for promotion to the vacancies which arose prior to the Rules in regard to the post of Inspector. The High Court also found that it was only when the Rules were made that the restructuring in the Department, to which the Cabinet gave its approval, came into effect. Regarding vacancies arising after Inspector Rules, 2002 came to be notified, it was left undecided.

Held, while dismissing the appeals:

i. Promotion to the post of Inspector was governed by the 1979 Rules till Inspector Rules, 2002 came to be notified.

ii. Under the 1979 Rules, Data Entry Operators were not among the feeder categories for promotion as Inspector.

iii. Cabinet approved restructuring of certain posts including the post of Inspector. The number of posts of Inspector fell. Thereunder, the post of Data Entry Operator Grade B among other categories, were merged and the cadre of Senior Tax Assistants emerged. However, the restructured cadre of Senior Tax Assistants, did not come into being.

iv. The restructured Cadre of Senior Tax Assistants was born with the bringing into force of the Senior Tax Assistant Rules 2003. Data Entry Operators Grade B, among other categories, were re-designated as Senior Tax Assistants under Rule 5.

v. The Inspector Rules 2002, was brought into force superseding the 1979 Rules relating to Inspectors.

vi. The post of Senior Tax Assistant, which was not among the feeder categories under the 1979 Rules, became one of the feeder categories for promotion as Inspector, under Inspector Rules, 2002 under Clause (b) of Column 12.

vii. There was a ban of promotion to the posts of Inspector. The communication establish that the Draft Recruitment Rules which were finalized and brought into force as far as Inspectors were concerned and Draft Recruitment Rules finalized and brought into force as far as Senior Tax Assistants were concerned, were to be basis for promotion to the post of Inspector. As per Order, Departmental Promotion Committee

(DPC), was to operate, based on the draft Rules but no promotion orders were to be issued till the draft Rules were finalized. Even the promotion orders were permitted. The authority apparently contemplated simultaneous bringing into force of the Inspector Rules and the STA Rules.

viii. The High Court was in error in holding that it has to be necessarily held that the vacancies which arose prior to the revised Recruitment Rules coming into force has to be filled-up under then existing Rules (the 1979 Rules) relying upon case law. There was a conscious decision taken to not fill-up vacancies based on the restructuring, and what was more, letters show that promotion to the post of Inspector was to be effected based on the new recruitment rules.

ix. It was while so, that in the Hyderabad Commissionerate, by Notice, persons falling under the Draft Inspector Rules who also corresponded to the feeder categories under the extant Statutory Rules, the 1979 Rules, alone were called for selection as Inspector.

x. The benefit of reckoning service under Note 1 to categories in Clause (a) would be available only after the restructuring came into effect. This also indicates that the powers that be contemplated simultaneous operation of the Inspector Rules and the Senior Tax Assistant Rules.

xi. Appellants were not entitled to have seniority determined in respect of vacancies of Inspector which arose prior to Inspector Rules, 2002 came to be notified. The Appellants were eligible to be considered for promotion from issuance of the Statutory Rules in the case of Senior Tax Assistants was published in the Official Gazette and they are entitled to add their service as Data Entry Operator Grade B for the purpose of the 2002 Inspector Rules and considered for vacancies to be filled by promotion, which arose after Inspector Rules, 2002 came to be notified. The persons in Clause (a) under Column 12 of the 2002 Rules, were also entitled to be considered for two years. Seniority was to be considered based on Rule 5 of the STA Rules. The exercise, as above, if not carried out already shall be carried out. Further promotions based on the above would be granted. However, this court direct that the promotions shall be notional where promotions have already been effected, however, entitling the parties to seniority and pensionary benefits.

CHAPTER FIVE

STATE OF U.P. AND ORS. VS. VIKASH KUMAR SINGH AND ORS.,2021

Hon'ble Judges/Coram:

M.R. Shah and B.V. Nagarathna, JJ.

Equivalent Citation: 2021(11)ADJ472, MANU/SC/1114/2021

Relevant sections: Rule 5(iii) and Rule 8(iii) of the U.P. Service of Engineers (Irrigation Department) (Group A) Service Rules, 1990

Number of pages in original Judgment: 04

Case Note:

Service - Promotion - Eligibility list - Chief Engineer (Civil) Level-II is governed by the U.P. Service of Engineers (Irrigation Department) (Group A) Service Rules, 1990 - U.P. Government Servants Relaxation in Qualifying Service for Promotion Rules, 2006 - Promotion of Superintending Engineers (Civil) to the post of Chief Engineer (Civil) Level-II - Impugned judgment confirmed the quashing and setting aside of subject eligibility lists - Hence, the present appeal by State

Brief Facts:

The Respondents/ original writ Petitioners claimed promotion to the post of Chief Engineer (Civil) Level-II. Since there were 26 vacancies of Chief Engineer determined, total 78 Superintending Engineers (Civil) were eligible to be considered for promotion to the post of Chief Engineer. Theoriginal writ Petitioners preferred Writ against the relevant eligibility lists on the ground that they were entitled to the relaxation in minimum qualifying service as per Relaxation Rules, 2006. The ld. Single Judge issued the writ of mandamus commanding the competent authority to prepare the eligibility list of Superintending Engineer (Civil) including the names of the original writ Petitioners for promotion to the post of Chief Engineer (Civil) granting them relaxation in minimum length of service in accordance with Relaxation Rules, 2006. Division Bench of the High Court confirmed the judgment and order passed by the learned Single Judge. Hence, the present appeal.

Held, while allowing the Appeal:

i. It is an admitted position that the original writ Petitioners did not fulfil the eligibility criteria as they did not have the qualifying service of having completed 25 years of service. Thus, the eligibility lists were prepared by the department absolutely as per Rule 5(iii) and Rule 8(iii) of the Rules, 1990. The names of the original writ Petitioners were excluded from the eligibility list of Superintending Engineer for promotion to the post of Chief Engineer on the ground that they did not fulfil the eligibility criteria as per Rule 5(iii) of the Rules, 1990. Therefore, as such, the High Court ought not to have set aside the said eligibility lists, which as such were prepared absolutely in accordance with the Rules, 1990.
ii. High Court has committed a grave error in issuing the writ of mandamus commanding the competent authority to grant relaxation in the qualifying service. Impugned judgments and orders passed by the learned Single Judge as well as the Division Bench of the High Court are not sustainable in law.
iii. Appeal allowed. The impugned judgment and order quashed and set aside.

CHAPTER SIX

Union of India (UOI) and Ors. Vs. N. Murugesan and Ors.,2021

Hon'ble Judges/Coram:

Sanjay Kishan Kaul and M.M. Sundresh, JJ.

Equivalent Citation: 2021(4)SCT287(SC), 2021(3)SLJ401(SC), MANU/SC/0809/2021

Relevant sections: CPRI (Pay, Recruitment and Promotion) Rules, 1989; Article 226 of the Constitution of India

Number of pages in original Judgment: 16

Case Note:

Service - Tenure based appointment - CPRI (Pay, Recruitment and Promotion) Rules, 1989 (Working Rule No. 1) - Appointment sought to be extended similar to regular employees - Request not heeded and private Respondent appointed - Writs filed challenging appointment and denial of extension dismissed - By impugned judgment Division Bench allowed appeals without granting reinstatement - Hence the present appeals - Whether impugned judgments not sustainable in view of the Rules in question?

Brief Facts:

By the Office Memorandum (OM), Government of India introduced a procedure for appointment of certain specified posts. Order of appointment was issued favouring Respondent and he accepted the offer. He joined his office. Series of representations made by Respondent while reaching end of tenure to the effect that appointment was made by way of direct recruitment, he should be treated as a regular employee and therefore to be continued till the date of his superannuation. However new recruitment was made. Respondent filed writs questioning the relieving order given to him by terming it as an order of termination with a further challenge to the recruitment of the private Respondent. Petitions were dismissed on the ground of delay and laches and that such case did not require invocation of discretionary jurisdiction under Article 226 of the Constitution. The Division Bench allowed the appeals without granting an order of reinstatement by compensating the Respondent. Other reliefs sought by the Respondent were not considered and granted. Against this order of the Division Bench, both the parties raised present appeal.

Held, while disposing the Appeals:

i. There is no element of an unequal bargaining power involved. Nobody has forced the Respondent to enter into a contract.
ii. On the principle governing delay, laches, and acquiescence, followed by approbation and reprobation, Respondent No. 1 ought not to have been granted any relief by invoking Article 226 of the Constitution of India. There is no prohibition in law for a tenure appointment. The Division Bench was not right in holding that the highest constitutional authority on the executive side was misled by the lower officials. A conscious decision has been made to go for a tenure appointment in the interest of society. Similarly, a conscious decision was also made to go for a fresh recruitment.
iii. In the absence of any prohibition and mandatory mode of appointment, the Appellant's decision in going for a tenure appointment is perfectly in order.
iv. The private Respondent has already been appointed after following the due procedure and continues to date. The Respondent is an ex-employee of the first Appellant-Society and, having put in 23 years of service, knows its functioning very well. Thus, the order passed by the Division Bench cannot be sustained in the eye of the law.
v. Appeals filed by the Respondent deserve to be dismissed. Respondent since not entitled to any extension, the consequential benefits cannot be granted.

vi. Appeals filed by the Appellants stand allowed by setting aside the impugned order under challenge, and as a consequence, the appeals filed by the Respondent dismissed.

CHAPTER SEVEN

Mukesh Kumar and Ors. Vs. The State of Uttarakhand and Ors., 2020

Hon'ble Judges/Coram:

L. Nageswara Rao and Hemant Gupta, JJ.

Equivalent Citation: AIR2020SC992, 2020(2)BLJ147, 2020(4)CTC605, 2020(I)CLR(SC)730, 2020(1)J.L.J.R.418, 2020(2)KarLJ242, 2020LabIC1574, 2020(3)LLN15(SC), 2020(4)MhLj338, 2020(4)MPLJ255, 2020(I)OLR519, 2020(1)PLJR462, (2020)3SCC1, (2020)1SCC(LS)433, 2020 (4) SCJ 387, 2020(1)SLJ350(SC), 2020(4)SLR930(SC), MANU/SC/0139/2020

Relevant sections: Articles 16 (4) and 16 (4-A) of Constitution of Indian; Section 3(7) of Uttar Pradesh Public Services Act, 1994

Number of pages in original Judgment: 07

Case Note:

Constitution - Reservations - Quantifiable data - Articles 16 (4) and 16 (4-A) of Constitution of Indian and Section 3(7) of Uttar Pradesh Public Services Act, 1994 - Section 3(7) of 1994 Act related with Government Orders providing reservation for appointment to public posts filled up by promotion - High Court declared Section 3(7) of 1994 Act unconstitutional and directed that no promotion could be given by State by taking recourse to Section 3(7) of Act - By way of implementation of judgment of High Court, committee was constituted by Government for collection of quantifiable data relating to backwardness of reserved communities in State and inadequacy of their representation in public posts - State Government decided that all posts in public services in State shall be filled up without providing any reservations to Scheduled Castes and Scheduled Tribes - Writ Petition was filed for quashing proceeding initiated by State Government - High Court struck down proceeding as being contrary to law - Respondents filed application for review of judgment passed by High Court - High Court clarified that State Government was obligated to collect quantifiable data regarding inadequacy of representation of Scheduled Castes and Scheduled Tribes in state services before providing reservation in promotion - Hence, present appeal - Whether State Government was bound to make reservations in public posts and decision by State Government not to provide reservations could be only on basis of quantifiable data was sustainable.

Brief Facts:

Section 3(7) of the 1994 Act, the Government Orders providing reservation for appointment to public posts filled up by promotion which were existing on the date of commencement of the 1994 Act shall continue till they are modified or revoked. The High Court declared Section 3(7) of the 1994 Act unconstitutional and directed that no promotion could be given by the State by taking recourse to Section 3(7) of the 1994 Act. The application filed for review of the judgment in Vinod Prakash Nautiyal was dismissed. By way of implementation of the judgment of the High Court, a committee was constituted by the Government for collection of quantifiable data relating to the backwardness of the reserved communities in the State and the inadequacy of their representation in public posts. The State Government decided that all posts in public services in the State shall be filled up without providing any reservations to Scheduled Castes and Scheduled Tribes. All Government Orders to the contrary were superseded by the proceeding. An writ petition was filed for quashing the proceeding. The High Court by its judgment struck down the proceeding as being contrary to the law. The High Court observed that it was not necessary for the State Government to collect quantifiable data regarding representation of Scheduled Castes and Scheduled Tribes in State services or regarding their backwardness before providing reservation in their favour in promotion posts. In the meanwhile, the Respondents filed an application for review of the judgment. The High Court clarified that the State Government was obligated to collect quantifiable data regarding inadequacy of representation of the Scheduled Castes and Scheduled Tribes in state services before providing reservation in promotion. The High Court clarified that it was not necessary for the State Government to collect data regarding backwardness of the Scheduled Castes and Scheduled Tribes in the light of the direction of this Court in Jarnail Singh. As such, the High Court directed the State Government to collect quantifiable data regarding inadequacy of the representation of the Scheduled Castes and Scheduled Tribes in Government services which would enable the State Government to take a considered decision on providing or not providing reservation. The State Government was directed to take a decision whether to provide reservation or not only after considering the data relating to the adequacy or inadequacy of representation of Scheduled Castes and Schedule Tribes in the services of the State.

Held, while disposing off the appeal:

i. The High Court committed an error by striking down the proceeding by which a decision was taken not to provide reservation in promotions without giving any reasons, except stating that the said decision was contrary to the judgments of this Court in Jarnail Singh and Indra Sawhney. A perusal of the proceeding would show that the decision taken by the State Government was by way of implementation of the judgment of the High Court in Vinod Prakash Nautiyal by which Section 3(7) of the 1994 Act, relating to the provision of reservation in promotion, was struck down. By its judgment in Vinod Prakash Nautiyal, the High Court declared Section 3(7) of the 1994 Act as contrary to the law laid down by this Court in M. Nagaraj. There was a further declaration that no promotion could be given by the State by taking recourse to Section 3(7) of the 1994 Act. However, the State Government was given liberty to bring out another legislation in accordance with the mandate of the Constitution of India, by following the judgment in M. Nagaraj. This Court dismissed the SLP filed against the said judgment. At this juncture, it was relevant to mention that certain notifications were issued after the formation of the State by which reservation in promotion to public posts as provided in the State was adapted with certain modifications. The Government of Uttarakhand appointed a Committee for collection of quantifiable data pertaining to the adequacy or inadequacy of representation of the members of Scheduled Castes and Scheduled Tribes in public services in the State. The Committee submitted its report, according to which the representation of Scheduled Castes and Scheduled Tribes was inadequate. The State Cabinet approved the recommendation of the Committee. Ultimately, the State Government by a proceeding decided to set aside all previous Government orders relating to reservation in promotions to Government services in the State. As the Government was not bound to provide reservation in promotions, there was no justifiable reason for the High Court to have declared the proceeding as illegal.

ii. The direction that was issued to the State Government to collect quantifiable data pertaining to the adequacy or inadequacy of representation of persons belonging to Scheduled Castes and Scheduled Tribes in Government services is the subject matter of challenge in some appeals before us. In view of the law laid down by this Court, there was no doubt that the State Government was not bound to make reservations. There was no fundamental right which inheres in an individual to claim reservation in promotions. No mandamus could be issued by the Court directing the State Government to provide reservations. It was abundantly clear from the judgments of this Court in Indra Sawhney, Ajit Singh (II), M. Nagaraj and Jarnail Singh that Article 16(4) and 16(4-A) are enabling provisions and the collection of quantifiable data showing inadequacy of representation of Scheduled Castes and Scheduled Tribes in public service is a sine qua non for providing reservations in promotions. The data to be collected by the State Government was only to justify reservation to be made in the matter of appointment or promotion to public posts, according to Article 16(4) and 16(4-A) of the Constitution. As such, collection of data regarding the inadequate representation of members of the Scheduled Castes and Schedules Tribes, was a pre requisite for providing reservations, and was not required when the State Government decided not to provide reservations. Not being bound to provide reservations in promotions, the State was not required to justify its decision on the basis of quantifiable data, showing that there was adequate representation of members of the Scheduled Castes and Schedules Tribes in State services. Even if the under-representation of Scheduled Castes and Schedules Tribes in public services was brought to the notice of this Court, no mandamus could be issued by this Court to the State Government to provide reservation in light of the law laid down by this Court in C.A.

Rajendran and Suresh Chand Gautam. Therefore, the direction given by the High Court that the State Government should first collect data regarding the adequacy or inadequacy of representation of Scheduled Castes and Scheduled Tribes in Government services on the basis of which the State Government should take a decision whether or not to provide reservation in promotion was contrary to the law laid down by this Court and was accordingly set aside. Yet another direction given by the High Court in its judgment directing that all future vacancies that are to be filled up by promotion in the posts of Assistant Engineer, should only be from the members of Scheduled Castes and Scheduled Tribes, was wholly unjustifiable and is hence set aside.

CHAPTER EIGHT

Registrar Karnataka University and Ors. Vs. Prabhugouda and Ors., 2020

Hon'ble Judges/Coram:

Ashok Bhushan, R. Subhash Reddy and M.R. Shah, JJ.

Equivalent Citation: 2021(1)ALT65, 2021(1)ESC73(SC), 2021(2)KarLJ193, 2021 (1) SCJ 84, 2021(1)SCT122(SC), 2020(Suppl.)Sim.L.C. 470, 2021(1)SLJ20(SC), 2021(2)SLR532(SC), MANU/SC/0952/2020

Relevant sections: Section 2(2) of Karnataka State Universities Act, 2000

Number of pages in original Judgment: 07

Case Note:

Service - Promotion - Determination of date - In pursuance of syndicate Resolution, first Respondent-Petitioner was appointed as Associate Professor in P.G. Department of Studies in Mathematics in University - By issuing Circular, University invited applications for promotion, from eligible Assistant Professors, Associate professor and Professor under CAS - First Respondent made application for promotion to post of Professor under UGC, CAS and promotion order was issued promoting writ Petitioner as Professor, with effect from date of his eligibility to said post - Claim of writ Petitioner, for grant of CAS promotion from date he had completed three years of service in cadre of Associate Professor was rejected - First Respondent had filed writ petition before High Court - Single Judge allowed writ petition, by recording finding that writ Petitioner completed three years of teaching by certain date and his service in affiliated College was also to be considered for purpose of promotion under CAS - Aggrieved by order of Single Judge, Appellants preferred writ appeal which was dismissed - Hence, present appeal - Whether effective date of Career Advancement Scheme (CAS) promotion of first Respondent-writ Petitioner was from date he had completed three years of service in cadre of Associate Professor.

Brief Facts:

The first Respondent-writ Petitioner was earlier working as an Associate Professor, in J.S.S. College, which is affiliated to Karnataka University. In pursuance of syndicate Resolution, the writ Petitioner was appointed as an Associate Professor in the P.G. Department of Studies in Mathematics in the University. By issuing Circular, the University invited applications for promotion, from eligible Assistant Professors, Associate professor and Professor under CAS. The first Respondent-writ Petitioner made an application in response to the said Circular, for promotion to the post of Professor under UGC, CAS. He appeared for interview before the Board of Appointment (BOA), which had recommended his case for promotion and accordingly promotion order was issued, promoting the writ Petitioner as a Professor, with effect from the date of his eligibility, to the said post. The claim of the writ Petitioner, for grant of CAS promotion from date he had completed three years of service in cadre of Associate Professor, was placed before the Syndicate of the University, and the Syndicate in its meeting had rejected the claim. Challenging the Resolution of the Syndicate of the University, the first Respondent had filed writ petition before the High Court. The Single Judge of the High Court allowed the writ petition, by recording a finding that the writ Petitioner completed three years of teaching. Single Judge of the High Court was of the view that his service in affiliated College was also to be considered for the purpose of promotion under CAS and consequently writ Petitioner is entitled for promotion from date he had completed three years of service in cadre of Associate Professor. Aggrieved by the Order of the learned Single Judge, the Appellants herein preferred the writ appeal, the said writ appeal was dismissed, confirming the Order of the Single Judge.

Held, while allowing the appeal:

i. The High Court, by losing sight of a vital aspect namely, that the first Respondent was not in actual service of the University or of the constituent College, had ordered to extend the benefit from date Appellant had completed three years of service in cadre of Associate Professor, on the ground that he had completed three years of service, by working as Assistant Professor in Mathematics in UGC pay scale. There could not be any promotion in the University for the period where the writ Petitioner was not in effective service of the University. The University was not expected to order promotion for the period when he was working in affiliated college. The High Court, by mere mathematical calculation, by basing on the service certificate before the High Court, had held that as he has completed three years of service as Assistant Professor in UGC scale and therefore the effective date of promotion should be from date he had completed three years of service in cadre of Associate Professor and not he became eligible to said post, as granted by the University. Further, the High Court had fell in error in interpreting clause, by giving liberal meaning to the word colleges, by extending to affiliated college. Even the Division Bench had also committed the same error by recording a finding that a magnanimous interpretation was to be given for the wordings University/Colleges, as used in the Statute. The University had correctly interpreted the various clauses of the Statute and by giving the benefit of past service, had given effect to his promotion from the date of entry into the service of the University. It was also to be noticed that at the time of appointment itself, though the writ Petitioner had completed three years of service, fully knowing that he was not eligible for appointment as a Professor, he had not claimed the post of Professor. Even the representations filed by the writ Petitioner indicate that he claimed notional service, in spite of the same, the High Court, by misconstruing the statute contrary to its objectives, as mentioned in the preamble liberally construed, going beyond the scope of the statute and granted all consequential benefits, by declaring that the effective date for promotion was to from date he had completed three years of service in cadre of Associate Professor.

ii. There was no substance in the argument made by the Respondents, that the term principals of Constituent Colleges ought to be read disjunctively as against the other posts mentioned in the provision. If it was to be read in the manner as sought to be argued by Counsel, same would run contrary to the objectives and preamble of the statute itself. Even the submission of the Counsel relying on the definition under Section 2(2) of Karnataka State Universities Act, 2000, also did not render any assistance to support his case. Karnataka State Universities Act, 2000, applies to all the colleges, which includes private college. Even private colleges have to seek affiliation from the jurisdictional University, as such the College is widely defined in the Act. Said definition cannot be readily imported, as defined, for the purpose of grant of promotions under CAS. For the purpose of grant of promotions under CAS, the word College was to be interpreted, keeping in mind, the preamble of the statute, governing promotions.

iii. The incumbent teacher, who was entitled for promotion under the scheme, was to be given benefit only from the entry of service of such incumbent into the University. Though the earlier service was to be counted for the purpose of giving benefit of promotion, but effective date for all purposes was only from the date of entry of first Respondent into the University service. The University was not expected to grant promotion, covering the period, anterior to the entry of service of the first Respondent into University. The University had rightly given the benefit of promotion from date he had completed three years of service in cadre of Associate Professor.

CHAPTER NINE

Union Public Service Commission Vs. Jawahar Santhkumar and Ors., 2019

Hon'ble Judges/Coram:

R. Banumathi, A.S. Bopanna and Hrishikesh Roy, JJ.

Equivalent Citation: 2019(6)ALT234, 2020(2)CWC164, 2020(1)ESC19(SC), 2020(3)LLN294(SC), (2020)1MLJ375, 2019(16)SCALE573, 2020(1)SCT79(SC), 2020(1)SLJ92(SC), 2020(1)SLR950(SC), MANU/SC/1578/2019

Relevant sections: Section 3 of All India Services Act, 1951; Regulation 5, 6 and 7 of Indian Administrative Service (Appointment by Promotion) Regulations, 1955

Number of pages in original Judgment: 10

Case Note:

Service - Promotion - Denial of - Meeting of Selection Committee for promotion to IAS was held in which first Respondent's name could not be included in Select List due to lower grading and also due to statutory limit on size of Select List - Aggrieved by his non-appointment to IAS, first Respondent filed original application before Administrative Tribunal - Said application was dismissed by Tribunal finding no irregularity by Selection Committee in making relative assessment - Aggrieved by dismissal of his application, first Respondent filed writ petition before High Court - High Court set aside order of Tribunal and directed Appellant and Respondent Nos. 2 and 3 to convene Selection Committee Meeting for reviewing promotions made to IAS and promote first Respondent to IAS from date when his juniors were promoted - Hence, present appeal - Whether High Court was right in directing Appellant to convene Review Selection Committee Meeting and promote first Respondent to IAS from date his juniors were promoted with all consequential benefits.

Brief Facts:

A meeting of the Selection Committee for promotion to the IAS against three vacancies as determined by the Central Government was held in which the first Respondent's name could not be included in the Select List due to lower grading and also due to the statutory limit on the size of the Select List. Aggrieved by his non-appointment to the IAS, the first Respondent filed OA No. 749 of 2006 before the Central Administrative Tribunal. The Tribunal found no irregularity by the Selection Committee in making the relative assessment, the Tribunal dismissed the application filed by the first Respondent. Aggrieved by the dismissal of his application, the first Respondent filed writ petition. The High Court set aside the order of the Tribunal by holding that the Selection Committee and the Tribunal failed to assess all the aspects of the case in their proper perspective and directed the Appellant and Respondent Nos. 2 and 3 to convene a Selection Committee Meeting for reviewing the promotions made to the IAS and promote the first Respondent to the IAS from the date when his juniors were promoted with all the consequential benefits.

Held, while allowing the appeal:

i. While assessing the suitability of the officers for promotion, the Selection Committee, as per the uniform and consistent practice followed in the matter of induction to the All India Services, examines the service records of each of the eligible officers, with special reference to the performance of the officers during the last five years (preceding the year for which the Select List was being prepared), deliberating on the quality of the officer as indicated in the various columns recorded by the reporting/reviewing/accepting authority in the ACRs for different years and then after detailed mutual deliberation and discussion, finally arrives at a classification to be assigned to each officer.

ii. Insofar as the present case, the first Respondent's name was included by the State Government in the list of officers eligible for consideration. Accordingly, the Selection Committee also considered the ACRs and made a relative assessment to all the officers under consideration. The name of the first Respondent could not be included in the Select List as the overall grading given to him by the Selection Committee was lower and there were only three vacancies. Since the name of the first Respondent could not be included in the Select List for promotion to the IAS Cadre, the first Respondent was not considered for promotion.

Neither the decision of the Selection Committee nor the decision-making process suffers from any arbitrariness. Since there was down-grading of the first Respondent, the first Respondent was not included in the Select List. On overall assessment of service records, the name of the first Respondent was not included in the Select List due to the statutory limit of its size and as officers with higher grading in the Select List were available as per the provisions of Regulation 5(5) of the Regulations. The High Court was not right in holding that the Selection Committee had miserably failed to assess all the aspects of the case in their proper perspective and that the promotions made to the IAS for the vacancies was vitiated and the same was to be reviewed. The impugned judgment of the High Court could not be sustained and was liable to be set aside.

CHAPTER TEN

GIRISH KUMAR VS. STATE OF MAHARASHTRA AND ORS., 2019

Hon'ble Judges/Coram:

L. Nageswara Rao and M.R. Shah, JJ.

Equivalent Citation: 2019(6)ALLMR1, 2019(4)BomCR25, 2019(2)ESC418(SC), 2019(4)LLN36(SC), 2019(8)SCALE281, (2019)6SCC647, 2019 (10) SCJ 187, 2019(3)SCT53(SC), 2019(4)SLR696(SC), MANU/SC/0743/2019

Relevant sections: Rule 5 of the Seniority Rules, 1982; Section 274 of Maharashtra Zilla Parishads and Panchayat Samities Act, 1961; Article 309 of Constitution of India, 1950

Number of pages in original Judgment: 07

Ratio Decidendi:

If any employee is granted the deemed date of promotion, his seniority shall be considered accordingly from that date

Case Note:

Service - Order of promotion - Legality - Rule 5 of the Seniority Rules, 1982 and Section 274 of Maharashtra Zilla Parishads and Panchayat Samities Act, 1961 and Article 309 of Constitution of India, 1950 and Appendix IX to the Maharashtra Zilla Parishads District Services (Recruitment) Rules, 1967 (Recruitment Rules, 1967) - Appellant had preferred present appeal against impugned order confirming order of promotion of Respondent No. 3 dated 1st February, 2008 - Whether an employee who had been assigned deemed date of promotion as per Rule 5 of Rules, 1982 and as such had not actually worked at all on promotional post, could it be said that he had completed service for a continuous period of not less than three years in feeder cadre, which was requirement under relevant Recruitment Rules.

Brief Facts:

It was the case on behalf of the Appellant that, the eligibility criteria as per the Maharashtra Zilla Parishads District Services (Recruitment) Rules, 1967 ('Recruitment Rules, 1967) for the post of Section Officer was 'continuous service of not less than three years' in the grade of Office Superintendent and Respondent No. 3 never completed his continuous service of not less than three years on the post of Office Superintendent, he was not eligible for promotion to the post of Section Officer. Vide order, the Additional Divisional Commissioner, allowed the said appeal preferred by the Appellant herein and quash and set aside the order of promotion of Respondent No. 3 to the post of Section Officer. Being aggrieved by the order passed by the Additional Divisional Commissioner, Respondent No. 3 preferred Writ Petition before the High Court. A learned Single Judge of the High Court allowed the said writ petition and set aside the order passed by the Additional Divisional Commissioner, and consequently confirmed the order of promotion of Respondent No. 3. Division Bench of the High Court has dismissed appeal and has confirmed the judgment and order passed by the learned Single Judge. Hence, the Appellant has preferred the present appeal.

Held, while allowing the appeal:

i. As per Appendix IX to the Recruitment Rules, 1967, no person shall be eligible for promotion unless he has completed service for a continuous period of not less than three years in District Service (Class III) (Ministerial) Grade II. Respondent No. 3 was promoted as Office Superintendent on 22nd October, 2007. However, he was granted deemed date of promotion under Rule 5 of the Seniority Rules, 1982 for promotion as Office Superintendent. He was promoted to the post of Section Officer on 1st February, 2008. The learned Single Judge and the Division Bench of the High Court have considered and applied the Seniority Rules, 1982 under which Respondent No. 3 was granted the deemed date of promotion. However, it is required to be noted that the

Seniority Rules, 1982 and the Recruitment Rules, 1967 both are different Rules and enacted under the different provisions and they operate in different fields. The Recruitment Rules, 1967 are enacted/framed in exercise of powers conferred by Clause xxxix of Sub-section 2 of Section 274 of Act, 1961. The said Rules shall apply to the recruitment to all posts in District Technical Service (Class III), District Service (Class III) and District Service (Class IV). On the other hand, the Seniority Rules, 1982 are framed/enacted in exercise of powers conferred by proviso to Article 309 of Constitution. As per the Seniority Rules, 1982, the seniority of government servants shall be regulated in accordance with the provisions of the Seniority Rules, 1982. The said Seniority Rules, 1982 are made applicable to the District Service also. Therefore, the Seniority Rules, 1982 shall govern the seniority only and not with respect to the recruitment. The recruitment shall be governed by the Recruitment Rules, 1967 only.

ii. In the present case, the High Court has considered Rule 5 of the Rules, 1982 and has not at all considered the Recruitment Rules, 1967. Respondent No. 3 might have been granted the deemed date of promotion to the post of Office Superintendent with effect from 7th October, 2005. However, he was actually promoted as Office Superintendent on 22nd October, 2007. Therefore, in fact, he has rendered service as Office Superintendent only from 22nd October, 2007. As per Appendix IX to the Recruitment rules, 1967, the eligibility for appointment to the promotional post of Section Officer requires three years continuous service. The language used in Appendix IX is unambiguous, simple and plain. Therefore, on a fair reading of Appendix IX of the Recruitment Rules, 1967, to become eligible for the promotional post of Section Officer, a person ought to have rendered continuous service of not less than three years. Continuous service might have been defined under the Seniority Rules, 1982. However, the same shall be for the purpose of seniority and the Seniority Rules only. Therefore, if any employee is granted the deemed date of promotion, his seniority shall be considered accordingly from the deemed date of promotion. However, that shall be only for the purpose of inter se seniority only and the same shall not be applicable while considering the eligibility criteria under the Recruitment Rules. In the Recruitment Rules, continuous service is not defined. While considering the relevant provisions and as per the Rule of interpretation, when the language used is unambiguous, plain and simple, the provision is required to be read as it is and nothing is to be added. Therefore, when in Appendix IX, the eligibility criteria is that no person shall be eligible for promotion unless he has completed service for a continuous service of not less than three years means he has to render/complete service for a continuous period of uninterrupted/unbroken three years service. Therefore, when Respondent No. 3 has not completed three years of service for a continuous period of not less than three years in the feeder cadre in District Service (Class III) (Ministerial) Grade II, he was not eligible for promotion to the post of Section Officer. The High Court has committed a grave error in holding otherwise. Therefore, the Additional Divisional Commissioner, rightly allowed the appeal and rightly set aside the order of promotion of Respondent No. 3 dated 1st February, 2008 to the post of Section Officer.

iii. Impugned judgments and orders passed by the learned Single Judge as well as the Division Bench of the High Court are hereby quashed and set aside and the order passed by the Additional Divisional Commissioner, is hereby restored. It is held that, Respondent No. 3 is not entitled to be promoted to the post of Section Officer and instead action should be taken to promote the Appellant to the post of Section Officer, as directed by the Additional Divisional Commissioner, Aurangabad. Appeal allowed.

CHAPTER ELEVEN

JARNAIL SINGH AND ORS. VS. LACHHMI NARAIN GUPTA AND ORS., 2018

Hon'ble Judges/Coram:

Dipak Misra, C.J.I., Kurian Joseph, Rohinton Fali Nariman, Sanjay Kishan Kaul and Indu Malhotra, JJ.

Equivalent Citation: AIR2018SC4729, 2018(6)ALT14, 2019 1 AWC605SC, 2018(4)BLJ225, 2018(II)CLR(SC)1224, [2020(165)FLR946], 2018(4)J.L.J.R.93, 2018(3)JLJ716, 2018(5)KarLJ689, 2018LabIC4509, (2018)7MLJ573, 2018(4)PLJR108, 2018(11)SCALE530, (2018)10SCC396, (2019)1SCC(LS)86, 2019 (2) SCJ 168, 2018(4)SCT445(SC), 2018(3)SLJ13(SC), 2019(2)SLR130(SC), (2020)1WBLR(SC)543, MANU/SC/1053/2018

Relevant sections: Articles 16, 341 and 342 of the Constitution of India

Number of pages in original Judgment: 22

Case Note:

Constitution - Reservation in promotion - Present reference filed for correctness of decision in M. Nagaraj v. Union of India which is in relation to equality of opportunity in matters of public employment - It had been argued that when case of Nagaraj states that State had to collect quantifiable data showing backwardness, such observation would be contrary to Indra Sawhney v. Union of India - Further, argued that creamy layer concept had not been applied in case of Indra Sawhney to Scheduled Castes and

Scheduled Tribes and case of Nagaraj had misread Indira Sawhney judgment to apply this concept to Scheduled Castes and the Scheduled Tribes - Whether impugned judgment of M. Nagaraj v. Union of India in relation to promotion in reservation warrant any interference.

Brief Facts:

The present reference had been filed for correctness of decision in M. Nagaraj v. Union of India which is in relation to equality of opportunity in matters of public employment. It had been argued that when Nagaraj states that the State has to collect quantifiable data showing backwardness, such observation would be contrary to the Indra Sawhney v. Union of India as it has been held therein that the Scheduled Castes and the Scheduled Tribes are the most backward among backward classes and it was, therefore, presumed that once they are contained in the Presidential List under Articles 341 and 342 of the Constitution of India, there was no question of showing backwardness of the Scheduled Castes and the Scheduled Tribes all over again. It was further argued that, the creamy layer concept had not been applied in Indra Sawhney to the Scheduled Castes and the Scheduled Tribes and Nagaraj had misread the said judgment to apply this concept to the Scheduled Castes and the Scheduled Tribes. Once the Scheduled Castes and the Scheduled Tribes had been set out in the Presidential List, they shall be deemed to be Scheduled Castes and Scheduled Tribes, and the said List could not be altered by anybody except Parliament under Articles 341 and 342 of Constitution of India.

Held, while answering the reference:

i. The reference to class in case of Nagaraj is to the Scheduled Castes and the Scheduled Tribes, and their inadequacy of representation in public employment. It was clear, therefore, that Nagaraj had, in unmistakable terms, stated that the State had to collect quantifiable data showing backwardness of the Scheduled Castes and the Scheduled Tribes. This Court was afraid that this portion of the judgment was directly contrary to the Indra Sawhney which had held that the test or requirement of social and educational backwardness cannot be applied to Scheduled Castes and Scheduled Tribes, who indubitably fall within the expression backward class of citizens.
ii. In fact, in case of E.V. Chinnaiah v. State of A.P. has referred to the Scheduled Castes as being the most backward among the backward

classes. This was for the reason that the Presidential List contains only those castes or groups or parts thereof, which had been regarded as untouchables. Similarly, the Presidential List of Scheduled Tribes only refers to those tribes in remote backward areas who are socially extremely backward. Thus, it was clear that when Nagaraj requires the States to collect quantifiable data on backwardness, insofar as Scheduled Castes and Scheduled Tribes were concerned, this would clearly be contrary to the Indra Sawhney and would have to be declared to be bad on this ground.

iii. When Nagaraj applied the creamy layer test to Scheduled Castes and Scheduled Tribes in exercise of application of the basic structure test to uphold the constitutional amendments leading to Articles 16(4-A) and 16(4-B), it did not in any manner interfere with Parliament's power under Article 341 or Article 342. Therefore, this part of the judgment did not need to be revisited.

iv. Nagaraj had wisely left the test for determining adequacy of representation in promotional posts to the States for the simple reason that as the post gets higher, it may be necessary, even if a proportionality test to the population as a whole is taken into account, to reduce the number of Scheduled Castes and Scheduled Tribes in promotional posts, as one goes upwards. This was for the simple reason that efficiency of administration has to be looked at every time promotions were made. As has been pointed in Indra Sawhney, there may be certain posts right at the top, where reservation is impermissible altogether. For this reason, it was clear that Article 16(4-A) of Constitution had been couched in language which would leave it to the States to determine adequate representation depending upon the promotional post that was in question.

v. Thus, the judgment in Nagaraj did not need to be referred to a seven-Judge Bench. However, the conclusion in Nagaraj that the State had to collect quantifiable data showing backwardness of the Scheduled Castes and the Scheduled Tribes, being contrary to the Indra Sawhney was held to be invalid to this extent.

CHAPTER TWELVE

Nawal Kishore Mishra and Ors. Vs. High Court of Judicature at Allahabad and Ors., 2015

Hon'ble Judges/Coram:

F.M. Ibrahim Kalifulla and Abhay Manohar Sapre, JJ.

Equivalent Citation: 2015III AD (S.C.) 596, AIR2015SC1332, 2015(3)ESC492(SC), 2015LabIC1498, 2015(3)LLN1(SC), (2015)3MLJ231(SC), 2015(2)SCALE506, (2015)5SCC479, (2015)2SCC(LS)168, 2015 (2) SCJ 430, 2015(2)SCT799(SC), 2015(2)SLJ66(SC), 2015(3)SLR481(SC), MANU/SC/0164/2015

Relevant sections: Rule 8(2) of Uttar Pradesh Higher Judicial Service Rule, 1975; Section 3(1) of Uttar Pradesh Public Services (Reservation) for Scheduled Casts and Scheduled Tribes and Other Backward Classes Act, 1994

Number of pages in original Judgment: 20

Case Note:

Service - Promotion - Appointment thereto - Rule 8(2) of Uttar Pradesh Higher Judicial Service Rule, 1975 and Section 3(1) of Uttar Pradesh Public Services (Reservation) for Scheduled Casts and Scheduled Tribes and Other

Backward Classes Act, 1994 - Division Bench dismissed Appellant's petition challenging appointment made by High Court to post of Direct Recruit District Judges in unfilled reserve vacancies, by way of promotion from 'in service candidates' by applying Rule 8(2) of Rules, 1975 - Hence, present appeal - Whether appointment made by promotion by applying Rule 8(2) of Rules was sustainable - Held, not in dispute that after special recruitment was made in respect of unfilled reserved vacancies, High Court proceeded to fill up all unfilled vacancies of direct recruits in reserved category and those posts were all filled up by promoting in-service candidates - High Court by adopting Reservation Act, 1994 adopted rule of reservation to full extent provided for and as prescribed under Section 3(1) of Reservation Act, 1994 - In respect of any unfilled vacancies of that category, High Court rightly resorted to prescription contained in Rule 8(2) by resorting to filling up of such vacancies by special recruitment in that year - Action of High Court in having resorted to filling up of unfilled reserved vacancies by taking umbrage under Rule 8(2) was perfectly justified - Such course adopted by High Court was in order, as proviso to Rule 8(2) specifically mandates that while fixing number of vacancies to be allotted to quota of direct recruitment at next recruitment, it should be raised accordingly - Appeal dismissed.

Brief Facts:

To trace the brief facts, on 15.04.2009 the High Court notified and called for applications for filling up 68 vacancies in the Higher Judicial Service. of the 68 vacancies, 24 vacancies were meant for open category, 21 for Other Backward Classes (OBC), 21 for SC and 2 for ST. It is not in dispute that all the 24 vacancies in the open category got filled up on merits. of the 21 vacancies in the OBC, 10 alone could be appointed leaving 11 vacancies to remain. All the SC/ST vacancies numbering 23 were also not filled up. In the unfilled 34 vacancies, the High Court promoted the 'in service candidates'. The Appellants were successful in the written test and also attended the interview. According to the Appellants, even applying Rule 8(2) of the Rules, all the 68 vacancies were direct recruit vacancies and that in the first instance, the unfilled vacancies should have been filled up only from the other successful candidates from the direct recruitment source. In other words, the contention was that only if no other successful candidate was available from the direct recruit source belonging to any of the categories, namely, open category or any other category such as OBC or SC/ST then and then alone the High Court could have resorted to promotion of 'in service candidates'. To put it differently, according to the Appellants since the posts advertised were by way of direct recruitment, it was meant for that particular source of recruitment, namely, "direct recruit" and all those successful candidates of that source alone, namely, 'direct recruit' were in the first instance eligible to be considered for being appointed to the unfilled posts of any of the categories, namely, open or OBC or SC or ST and in the event of unavailability of any candidate from that source then and then alone the High Court could have resorted to filling up of those posts by way of promotion of 'in service candidates'. Since, the above submission of the Appellants did not find favour with the High Court, the Appellants are before us.

Held, while dismissing the petition:

Keeping the said legal principle relating to applicability of Section 3(1) of the Reservation Act, 1994 vis-à-vis Rules 7 and 8(2) of the High Court Rules in mind, when we consider the last of the submissions made on behalf of the Appellants, it must be held that the action of the High Court in having resorted to filling up of the unfilled reserved vacancies by taking umbrage Under Rule 8(2) was perfectly justified. The said action of the High Court in having filled up those unfilled reserved vacancies of direct recruitment of the year 2009 was stated to have been made by promoting the in-service candidates. Though we have found that such a course adopted by the High Court was in order, as the proviso to Rule 8(2) specifically mandates that while fixing the number of vacancies to be allotted to the quota of direct recruitment at the next recruitment, it should be raised accordingly. We are of the view, without disturbing whatever promotions already made by resorting to Rule 8(2), the High Court can be permitted to provide that number of vacancies which remained unfilled in the year 2009 in the reserved category of direct recruit source by adding that number of vacancies in the recruitment to be made in the future years until such number of vacancies of unfilled reserved category pertaining to 2009 are filled.

66. With the above limited directions to the High Court, we do not wish to meddle with the promotions already made. We do not find any scope for granting any relief to the Appellants, as none of the submissions raised on behalf of the Appellants, which were though not considered by the Division Bench of the High Court and which were also dealt with by us in extenso and we find no merit. These appeals, therefore, fail and the same are accordingly dismissed.

CHAPTER THIRTEEN

HC Pradeep Kumar Rai and Ors. Vs. Dinesh Kumar Pandey and Ors., 2015

Hon'ble Judges/Coram:

Ranjan Gogoi and Pinaki Chandra Ghose, JJ.

Equivalent Citation: AIR2015SC2342, 2015(4) ALJ 478, 2015 (4) AWC 3780 (SC), 2015(2)LLN553(SC), (2015)5MLJ98(SC), 2015(6)SCALE238, (2015)11SCC493, 2015 (6) SCJ 603, 2015(3)SCT83(SC), 2015(6)SLR498(SC), 2015(3)UC1662, (2016)1UPLBEC621, MANU/SC/0588/2015

Relevant sections: Regulation 445 of Regulations of UP Government

Number of pages in original Judgment: 06

Case Note:

Service - Selection and promotion - Uttar Pradesh Police Regulations, 1976 - Present appeals filed against controversy relating to selection and promotion process in State viz-a-viz State Regulations and Government Order - Whether Regulations could prevail over or co-exist with Government Order - Held, as per Regulations four times candidates to number of vacancies, in marker cadet should be called for interview - Whereas, as per Government Order candidates securing 40% of marks in exam and 50% in total aggregate were to be called for interview process

- If both rules were to exist, it would create contradictory situation - Regulations are not superior law as compared to Government Orders - Regulations could prevail over or co-exist with Government Order regarding number of candidates to be called for interview - Even Appellants did not establish that had they been called for interview in category of four times number of vacancies, they would have been short listed - Moreover, present appeals were filed only by unsuccessful candidates after long gap and declaration of interview result - Further, sealed cover procedure followed in selection could not prejudice any candidate - Furthermore, non-awarding of separate marks by panelists on interview committee cannot be ground to quash entire process - There was no oblique motive or any miscarriage of justice warranting interference - Appeals dismissed.

Brief Facts:

The facts necessary for disposal of this case are that the Government of Uttar Pradesh took a decision on 23.01.1999 for recruitment of departmental candidates to the posts of Sub-inspectors in the State, both by direct recruitment and by promotion of Constables and head Constables. In continuation of the order dated 23.01.1999, another Government Order was issued on 3.02.1999, according to which all the vacancies of Sub-inspectors till 31.12.1999 were to be filled up. On 27.02.1999, the Government of Uttar Pradesh issued another Order which superseded the earlier Order dated 23.01.1999. The 27.02.1999 order provided a complete pattern of the examination and process of selection and promotion. As per the new pattern the promotion process was to be conducted in three steps:

i. The preliminary written examination and infantry test/physical test;
ii. Main written Examination; and
iii. Interview. Candidates who qualified the preliminary examination and IT/PT were eligible to appear in the main written examination.

As per the existing rules in 1999, 50% of total vacancies were to be filled up by promotion of persons serving as Constables and Head Constables and the remaining 50% vacancies were to be filled up by direct recruitment. It appears that at the time the selection process began, there were 2956 vacancies of the rank of Sub-inspectors in the State. So initially the number of vacancies for promotees quota were 1478. However, It appears that vide order dated 10.01.2000, another 86 posts were added to the promotees quota to be filled up by the departmental examination in pursuance of the direction made by State Backward Classes Commission, to maintain the ratio of promotees and direct recruits at the rate of 50%. Thus, the number of vacancies for promotees quota became 1564. It is to be noted that pursuant to the Division Bench judgment of the High Court of Allahabad in Special Appeal No. 1372 of 1999: ***State of Uttar Pradesh v. Ranbir Singh, the Government of Uttar Pradesh*** created another class of promotees which consisted of 385 Head Constables who were to be promoted directly by virtue of the length of their service without undergoing the selection process. The creation of this class is not contended before us and that controversy is settled by prior litigation. Thus, eventually it appears that total vacancies for people who were to be promoted after the selection process was 1176.

The preliminary test was held on 05.09.1999 and the result was announced on 05.11.1999 and those who qualified the preliminary test were permitted to appear in IT/PT which was held in December 1999. The result of IT/PT test was declared on 11.02.2000, which was challenged before the High Court of Allahabad in Writ Petition No. 9694/2000: ***Triloki Nath Pandey and Ors. v. State of Uttar Pradesh***, and the entire process was stayed till the conclusion of litigation. Thus, at the end of that round of litigation the State of Uttar Pradesh was directed to go ahead with the selection procedure. Government Notification for the main written examination was issued on 9.12.2004 and the main written examination was conducted on 25.12.2005. Result of the main written test was declared on 24.01.2006 and pursuant thereto, 9671 candidates were called for interview. The interviews were held at four centres between 15.05.2006 to 20.07.2006. The results of the interviews were made available on 11.11.2006.

It was after the declaration of the result of interview that the present round of litigation began, whereby the unsuccessful candidates challenged the interview process on several grounds. Initially the writ petition was filed before the Allahabad High Court, Lucknow Bench, which allowed the petition and directed the State to conduct fresh interview for the 1176 vacancies of the rank of Sub-Inspectors. The Division Bench of the Allahabad High Court allowed the appeal filed by the State Government, thus, reversing the judgment of the learned Single Judge. The Division Bench directed the State to appoint the candidates who were selected after the interview already held, for the rank of Sub-Inspectors.

Held, while dismissing the appeal:

Now, so far as the question of awarding consolidated marks by all the panelists in the interview is concerned, we are in agreement with the finding of the learned Single Judge. The purpose of constituting multi member interview panel is to remove the arbitrariness and ensure objectivity. It is required by each member of the interview panel to apply his/her own mind in giving marks to the candidates. The best evidence of independent application of mind by each panelist is that they awarded separate marks. However, if only consolidated marks are awarded at the interview, it becomes questionable, though not conclusive, whether each panelist applied his/her own mind independently. Having said that, we note that this Court cautioned in ***Lila Dhar v. State of Rajasthan and Ors.*** MANU/SC/0063/1981 : (1981) 4 SCC 159, that it is not for the Courts to re-determine the appropriate method of selection unless obvious oblique motives are proved in a particular case. Even in Lila Dhar's case (supra), the issue was regarding the marks awarded by the Selection Committee as one consolidated marks; the Court refused to interfere with the appointment process on this ground. Only because the panelists on the interview committee did not award separate marks, cannot be a ground to quash the entire process. Also, with respect to the legal argument that the Government Order dated 03.02.1999 provided that the marks must be separately awarded by interview panelists, we hold that the Government Order dated 3.02.1999 was in continuation of the Government Order dated 23.01.1999, which was superseded expressly by Government Order dated 27.02.1999. The Government Order dated 27.02.1999 did not provide any condition that the marks were to be separately awarded by each interview panelist. Thus, it cannot be argued that the Government did not follow the rules framed by itself.

Further, it is a settled law that in cases like the present one, where an Executive action of the State is challenged, Court must tread with caution and not overstep its limits. The interference by Court is warranted only when there are oblique motives or there is miscarriage of justice. In the present case, there is no oblique motive or any miscarriage of justice warranting interference by this Court. Hence, the appeals and the writ petition are dismissed.

CHAPTER FOURTEEN

PANCHRAJ TIWARI VS. M.P. STATE ELECTRICITY BOARD AND ORS., 2014

Hon'ble Judges/Coram:

H.L. Gokhale and Kurian Joseph, JJ.

Equivalent Citation: 2014iv AD (S.C.) 121, 2014(3)ALLMR430, 2014 (3) AWC 2386 (SC), 2014(1)ESC110(SC), [2014(141)FLR288], 2014LabIC2660, 2014(3)LLN310(SC), (2014)2MLJ764, 2014(3)MPHT117, 2014(II)MPJR(SC)178, 2014(3)SCALE401, (2014)5SCC101, (2014)2SCC(LS)119, 2014 (3) SCJ 164, 2014(2)SCT332(SC), 2014(2)SLJ117(SC), 2014(6)SLR227(SC), (2015)3WBLR(SC)49, MANU/SC/0178/2014

Relevant sections: Article 14 and 16 of the Constitution of India

Number of pages in original Judgment: 05

Case Note:

Employment - Promotion--Appellant, Junior Engineer in Rural Electricity Co-operative Society--Rural Electricity Co-operative Society completely merged with M.P. State Electricity Board--Employees of Rural Electricity Co-operative Society taken over and absorbed in M.P. State Electricity Board--Once service gets merged with another service, employees concerned has right to get positioned appropriately in merged service--M.P. State Electricity Board having absorbed appellant and other employees, cannot maintain stand that even after absorption they will retain distinct identity in equated cadre without any promotion as enjoyed by their compeers in parent service--On integration/merger/amalgamation it is not permissible to have complete denial of promotion forever in integrated service--Complete denial of promotion forever cannot be comprehended under constitutional scheme of Articles 14 and 16 of the Constitution--Impugned judgment set aside--Appellant entitled to retrospective pre-options at par with and with effect from dates on which Junior-most graduate engineer in parent service on date of absorption obtained such promotions.(2) Employment - Promotion--Chances of promotion are not conditions of service--But negation of even chance of promotion certainly amounts to variation in conditions of service attracting infraction of Articles 14 and 16 of the Constitution--If after integration, only chances of promotion are affected, it would have been only case of heart burn of individual or few individual which is only to be ignored.(3) Employment - Seniority--No employee has right to particular position in seniority list--But all employees have right to seniority since same forms basis of promotion--Employee has always interest to seniority and right to be considered for promotion.

Brief Facts:

Appellant a graduate started his career as junior engineer on 23.09.1986 in the Rural Electricity Cooperative Society, Rewa. During 1995, it appears a policy decision was taken by the State Government to dissolve all such societies and merge the same with Madhya Pradesh State Electricity Board (hereinafter referred to as 'MPSEB'). Accordingly, the Managing Committee of the Rural Electricity Cooperative Society, Rewa was superseded in May, 1995 and a Superintending Engineer of the MPSEB was appointed as Officer In-charge. However, it took a few years to complete the formalities of the merger. Finally the Rural Electricity Cooperative Society, Rewa was completely merged with the MPSEB w.e.f. 15.03.2002.

3. The principles of merger were clarified by the MPSEB after prolonged correspondence as per Annexure P-12 dated 15.06.2004. For the purpose of ready reference, we shall extract the contents:

'Please refer to this office order cited under reference. It is requested to issue necessary orders for absorption of employees of REC societies falling under your area of jurisdiction on the same terms & conditions of the societies. The terms & conditions of the societies may be obtained from DE (STC), Jabalpur.'

Held, while allowing the petition:

In the above circumstances, we set aside the judgment in appeal. The absorbed employees of the Rural Electricity Cooperative Societies, having due regard to their date of appointment/promotion in each category in the respective societies, shall be placed with effect from the date of absorption, viz., 15.03.2002 as juniors to the junior-most employee of the Electricity Board in the respective category. Thereafter, they shall be considered for further promotions as per the rules/Regulations of the MPSEB. All other principles/conditions of absorption shall remain as such. However, it is made clear that on such promotions, in the exigencies of service, the employee concerned would also be liable to be transferred out of the circle, if so required.

The Appellant accordingly shall be entitled to retrospective promotions at par with and with effect from the dates on which the junior-most graduate engineer in the parent service on the date of absorption obtained such promotions. However, we make it clear that benefits till date need to be worked out only notionally. The appeal is allowed as above. There is no order as to costs.

CHAPTER FIFTEEN

MANOJ MANU AND ORS. VS. UNION OF INDIA (UOI) AND ORS., 2013

Hon'ble Judges/Coram:

Anil R. Dave and A.K. Sikri, JJ.

Equivalent Citation: 2014(1)AJR741, 2014(2) CHN (SC) 106, 2013(4)ESC664(SC), [2013(139)FLR475], 2013(3)J.L.J.R.570, JT2013(11)SC374, 2014LabIC1075, 2013(4)LLN21(SC), 2013(4)PLJR88, 2013(10)SCALE204, (2013)12SCC171, (2014)2SCC(LS)706, 2013(4)SCT532(SC), 2013(114)SLJ351(SC), 2013(5)SLR653(SC), (2013)4UPLBEC2740, MANU/SC/0782/2013

Relevant sections: Article 14 and 16 of the Constitution of India; Section 19 of the Administrative Tribunal Act

Number of pages in original Judgment: 06

Case Note:

Service - Promotion - Appellants appeared in Limited Departmental Competitive Examination conducted by Union Public Service Commission (UPSC) for the next promotion on the requisition sent to it for 184 general category posts by the Department of Personnel and Training (DoP&T) - UPSC after holding exams recommended 184 candidates out of which 6 did not join - DoP&T forwarded requisitioned 6 general category vacancies, however, UPSC recommended names of 3 candidates from the reserve list maintained by it - Appellants who were next in the merit list secured same marks as another candidate recommended - Appellants alleged UPSC of acting in an arbitrary and discriminatory manner in contravention of Article 14 and 16 of the Constitution of India whereby denying them the right to get the appointment to the post to which they were not only selected but equally placed as another candidate who was given the appointment - Held, it was not the case where any of the persons initially joined and thereafter resigned/left/promoted etc. thereby creating the vacancies again - In such situation UPSC would have been right in not forwarding the names from the list as there is culmination of the process with the exhaustion of the notified vacancies and vacancies arising thereafter have to be filled up by fresh examination - In the instant case, out of persons recommended, six persons did not join at all - In these circumstances when the candidates in reserved list on the basis of examination already held, were available and DoP&T had approached UPSC "within a reasonable time" to send the names, there was no reason or justification on the part of the UPSC for not sending the names - Appeal was accordingly allowed and Mandamus was issued to UPSC to forward the names of the next three candidates to the DoP&T for appointment to the relevant post Service - Right to appointment - Whether by mere presence of name of the candidate in the select list entitles such candidate to claim right to appointment - Held, merely because the name of a candidate finds place in the select list, it would not give him/her indefeasible right to get appointment as well - It is always open to the Government not to fill up all vacancies, however, such decision should not be arbitrary or unreasonable - Once, the decision is found to be based on some valid reason, the Court would not issue any Mandamus to Government to fill up the vacancies.

Brief Facts:

This appeal has been preferred by the present Appellants questioning the validity of the judgment and order dated May 16, 2011 passed by the High Court, in Writ Petition which was filed by the Appellants questioning the validity of the order dated 29th March 2011, of the Central Administrative Tribunal (hereinafter referred to as the "Tribunal"), Principal Bench, New Delhi. The Tribunal had dismissed the Original Application preferred by the Appellants herein under Section 19 of the Administrative Tribunal Act against their non-appointment to the post of Section Officer's Grade of the Central Secretariat Service. The said O.A. was dismissed by the Tribunal vide order dated 29th March 2011 which has been upheld by the High Court.

There is no dispute about the facts, which may be briefly recapitulated to understand the controversy that has arisen in these proceedings. The Appellants were working as Assistants in the Central Secretariat Service (CSS) and appeared in Limited Departmental Competitive Examination for the next promotion to the post of Section Officer's Grade in that service. There are two channels of promotion: one by way of seniority and other fast track in the form of Limited Departmental Competitive Examination (LDCE). The Appellants appeared in the said LDCE 2005, which was conducted by the Union Public Service Commission (UPSC) on the requisition sent to it for 184 general category posts by the Department of Personnel and Training (DoP&T). After holding the examination the UPSC had recommended 184 candidates in two lots. First lot of 141 candidates who were found suitable candidates for the said post whereas in the second lot 43 successful candidates were recommended for appointment. Out of them 6 candidates did not join. The DoP&T thereafter vide its letter dated 20th November 2009 had requisitioned 6 general category vacancies. However, the UPSC recommended names of three candidates from out of reserve list maintained by it. These two Appellants who were next in the merit list had secured 305 marks, same as secured by one Rajesh Kumar Yadav who was recommended by the UPSC in the supplementary list candidates.

Held,

We are, therefore, of the opinion in the facts of the present case, the decision of UPSC in forwarding three names against requisition of DoP&T for six vacancies was inappropriate. We, accordingly, allow the present appeal; set aside the order of the High Court as well as Tribunal and issue Mandamus to the UPSC to forward the names of the next three candidates to the DoP&T for appointment to the post of Section Officer's Grade. They shall get the seniority from the date when Rajesh Kumar Yadav was appointed to the said post. Their pay shall notionally be fixed, without any arrears of the pay and other allowances. No costs.

CHAPTER SIXTEEN

State of Rajasthan Vs. Ucchab Lal Chhanwal, 2013

Hon'ble Judges/Coram:

Anil R. Dave and Dipak Misra, JJ.

Equivalent Citation: 2013XI AD (S.C.) 253, 2014(1)J.L.J.R.159, JT2013(14)SC255, 2013(5)LLN1(SC), 2014(1)PLJR350, 2013(13)SCALE272, (2014)1SCC144, (2014)1SCC(LS)34, 2014(1)SCT342(SC), 2014(1)SLJ232(SC), 2014(1)SLR395(SC), 2014 (1) WLN 5 (SC), MANU/SC/1105/2013

Relevant sections: Rajasthan Police Service Rules, 1954

Number of pages in original Judgment: 04

Case Note:

Service - Promotion - On the recommendations of Departmental Promotion Committee (DPC) persons junior to the Respondent were promoted - Promotion was bases on the criterion of seniority-cum-merit - DPC though considered the case of the Respondent, yet his case was not recommended for promotion for the vacancy as he was imposed with the punishment of censure however, he was promoted thereafter in the subsequent year - Respondent challenged this before the Writ Court which held that the promotion of the Respondent could not have been deferred as the seniority was required to be given more weightage over the merit - State in the appeal, circular dated 26.7.2006 which sets out certain guidelines relating to the types of punishments and their impact/effect on promotion of a personnel as per which the Respondent was found unfit to be promoted was pressed into service - Division Bench in appeal affirmed the order passed by Ld. Single Judge holding that the circular was not applicable as the controversy relating to promotion pertained to the year 1996-97 - Hence the present appeal - Held, finding recorded by the High Court pertaining to the circular held to be correct and unassailable - In the instant case the dispute related to promotion which would have impact on inter se seniority - Directions issued by the writ court as well as the Division bench pertaining to grant of promotion to the Respondents quashed - Appeals allowed in part and the order passed by the Division Bench as well as by the writ court set aside to the extent directions were issued granting benefit of promotion to the Respondent.

Brief Facts:

The Respondent was appointed in Rajasthan Police Service (Junior Scale) after his selection through Rajasthan Public Service Commission (for short "the Commission") vide order dated 19.10.1989. As stipulated in Rajasthan Police Service Rules, 1954 (for short "the Rules") the R.P.S. cadre is divided into four categories and the lowest category is in the junior scale. The persons from the junior Scale are promoted to senior scale and thereafter to super time scale. The Rules provide that the person who has six years experience in junior scale becomes eligible for consideration to senior scale. A seniority list was published on 19.8.1997 wherein the name of the Respondent found place at serial number 51 in junior scale. In respect of vacancies in the promotional posts arising against the quota of 1996-97 a Departmental Promotion Committee (DPC) was convened and on the basis of recommendations of the DPC persons junior to the Respondent were promoted. It is apt to mention here that the criterion for promotion was seniority-cum-merit.

Be it noted, the DPC though considered the case of the Respondent, yet his case was not recommended for promotion for the vacancy occurring in 1996-97 as he was imposed with the punishment of censure on 1.12.1992. However, he was promoted thereafter in the year 1998. In this backdrop the Respondent approached the High Court by way of filing S.B. Civil Writ Petition No. 6574 of 1997 for quashing of the penalty of censure imposed on him on 1.12.1992 and further for setting aside the order dated 22.8.1997 whereby he had been superseded and his juniors had been promoted. A prayer was made for issue of a direction to consider his candidature for promotion to the post of senior scale in Rajasthan Police Service and, if he was found suitable, to promote him with all consequential benefits.

Held, while allowing the appeal in part:

In the case at hand the dispute relates to promotion which will have impact on inter se seniority. The learned Counsel for the Respondents assiduously endeavoured to convince us that they are agitating the grievance with regard to their promotion and it has nothing to do with the persons junior to them who had been promoted. Despite the indefatigable effort, we are not persuaded to accept the aforesaid preponement, for once the Respondents are promoted, the juniors who have been promoted earlier would become juniors in the promotional cadre, and they being not arrayed as parties in the lis, an adverse order cannot be passed against them as that would go against the basic tenet of the principles of natural justice. On this singular ground the directions issued by the writ court as well as the Division bench pertaining to grant of promotion to the Respondents are quashed. To elaborate, as far as the conclusion of the High Court relating the circular is concerned, it is unexceptionable and we concur with the same.

Consequently, the appeals are allowed in part and the order passed by the Division Bench as well as by the writ court is set aside to the extent directions have been issued granting benefit of promotion to the Respondents. In the facts and circumstances of the case, there shall be no order as to costs.

CHAPTER SEVENTEEN

Debabrata Dash and Ors. Vs. Jatindra Prasad Das and Ors., 2013

Hon'ble Judges/Coram:

R.M. Lodha, Jasti Chelameswar and Madan B. Lokur, JJ.

Equivalent Citation: 2013IV AD (S.C.) 101, AIR2013SC1700, 2013(3)ALT12, 2013(3)ALT17, [2013(137)FLR576], [2013(137)FLR577], JT2013(8)SC384, 2013LabIC2695, 2013(5)LLN75(SC), (2013)3MLJ347, 2013(3)MPHT1, 2013(II)OLR73, 2013(3)SCALE378, (2013)3SCC658, (2013)1SCC(LS)751, [2013]2SCR331, 2013(2)SCT642(SC), 2013(2)SLJ306(SC), 2013(4)SLR456(SC), MANU/SC/0225/2013

Relevant sections: Rules 3(d), 4, 5, 7, 8 and 9 of Orissa Superior Judicial Service Rules, 1963; Orissa Judicial Service (Special Schemes) Rules, 2001

Number of pages in original Judgment: 12

Case Note:

Orissa Superior Judicial Service Rules, 1963 - Rules 3(d), 4, 5, 7, 8 and 9 - Orissa Judicial Service (Special Schemes) Rules, 2001 - Inter-se Seniority - Writ petitioners and appellants - Writ petitioner posted as an ad hoc Additional District Judge in the Fast Track Court on 26.04.2002 and allowed to officiate in the Senior Branch of the Superior Judicial Service on regular basis, joined on 03.02.2004 - Appellants being appointed in the Senior Branch cadre of Orissa Superior Judicial Service by way of direct recruitment and joined on 3.2.2003 and 7.2.2003 respectively - Whether promotion of the writ petitioner as an Ad hoc Additional District Judge can be said to be an appointment in the Senior Branch Cadre of Superior Judicial Service? - In the absence of any vacancy in the Senior Branch cadre of Superior Judicial Service to be filled up by promotion, no appointment to the Senior Branch of Service by way of promotion can be made - A person can become a member of the Senior Branch of the Superior Judicial Service only if his appointment has been made to a post in the service - if there is no vacancy to be filled in by promotion in the cadre of Senior Branch service, there is no question of any appointment being made to the service - The membership of service is limited to the persons who are appointed within the cadre strength by direct recruitment and by promotion - Petitioner's promotion as an Ad hoc Additional District Judge is traceable wholly and squarely to the 2001 Rules and not traceable to the 1963 Rules.2. Orissa Superior Judicial Service Rules, 1963 - Rules 7, 8 and 9 - Writ petitioner posted as an Ad hoc Additional District Judge in the Fast Track Court who joined on 26.04.2002 - Writ petitioner on posting as Additional District and Sessions Judge joined on 3.2.2004 - He submitted a representation to the High Court on administrative side seeking seniority in the cadre of District Judge w.e.f. 26.04.2002 - The claim of seniority by the Writ petitioner over and above the appellants was based on the ground that the period of his service as an Ad hoc Additional District Judge (Fast Track Court) should be included for the purpose of computing his length of service in the cadre of Senior Branch, Superior Judicial Service under the 1963 Rules - Full Court of the High Court rejected the representation of the writ petitioner - Division Bench has held that the promotion of the writ petitioner to the Senior Branch has to be counted w.e.f. 26.04.2002 when he joined the post initially and his subsequent regularization deserves to be considered to be effective from that date - Appeal - Writ petitioner's appointment as an Ad hoc Additional District Judge is not traceable to the 1963 Rules - Held, administrative decision by the Full Court is in accord with the 1963 Rules, the 2001 Rules - View of the Division Bench in the impugned judgment is legally unsustainable - Impugned judgment is liable to be set aside and is set aside.

Brief Facts:

The writ Petitioner joined the judicial service in the State of Orissa as Munsiff on probation on 15.07.1981 under the Orissa Judicial Service Rules, 1964. He was promoted to the Junior Branch of the Superior Judicial Service on 19.07.1999. On 05.01.2002, the writ Petitioner, who was continuing as a member of Superior Judicial Service (Junior Branch), was appointed, on ad hoc basis, as Additional District Judge in the Fast Track Court. Pursuant to the above order of appointment, on 11.04.2002 writ Petitioner was posted as an ad hoc Additional District Judge in the Fast Track Court at Bargarh where he joined on 26.04.2002.

On 13.01.2003, the Appellants were appointed in the Senior Branch cadre of Orissa Superior Judicial Service by way of direct recruitment under the 1963 Rules. Pursuant to the posting order dated 22.01.2003, they joined as Additional District and Sessions Judges at Cuttack and Behrampur on 03.02.2003 and 07.02.2003 respectively.

Held, while allowing the appeal:

We have already indicated above that on 05.01.2002 or 26.04.2002, there was no vacancy in the cadre of Superior Judicial Service (Senior Branch) for being filled up by promotion. Such vacancy in the Senior Branch cadre of the service occurred on 15.12.2003 and from that date the writ Petitioner has been given benefit of his service rendered in the Fast Track Court. The administrative decision by the Full Court is in accord with the 1963 Rules, the 2001 Rules and the legal position already indicated above. The view of the Division Bench in the impugned judgment is legally unsustainable. The impugned judgment is liable to be set aside and is set aside. Appeal is allowed, as above, with no order as to costs.

CHAPTER EIGHTEEN

Tamil Nadu Rural Development Engineers Association Vs. The Secretary to Government Rural Development Department and Ors., 2013

Hon'ble Judges/Coram:

S.S. Nijjar and M.Y. Eqbal, JJ.

Equivalent Citation: AIR2014SC159, 2014(1)AJR368, JT2014(1)SC245, 2014LabIC1514, (2013)7MLJ263, 2013(12)SCALE246, (2013)15SCC380, [2013]9SCR840, 2014(1)SCT610(SC), 2014(1)SLR788(SC), (2014)1WBLR(SC)844, MANU/SC/0993/2013

Relevant sections: Article 309 of the Constitution of India

Number of pages in original Judgment: 10

Case Note:

Service - Claim of absorption and promotion - Members of the Appellant-Association were initially appointed as Overseers by the then Highways and Rural Works Department (department) - A separate wing was later created in the Rural Development Department (RD) created and temporary appointment were made - Owing to further need of staff, State issued orders for absorption and recruitment of the Engineering Staff - Appellants at this point of time were occupying the posts of Overseer in the Highways Department but on temporary service in the RD Department - Appellants were given an opportunity to be permanently absorbed in the RD Department, by seeking their option and on the basis of Appellants exercising their option, were absorbed in the RD Department - Claim of Appellants under determination - Held, Appellants having voluntarily opted to be absorbed in the RD Department, without any protection of their previous service, cannot now be permitted to make a grievance that they have not been treated at par with the Direct Recruits - Direct Recruits joined on the post of AE - Appellants, even though some of them possessed the degree qualification, were absorbed on the post of Overseer - They were working on the post of Overseer in the Highways Department, the parent Department, even though they were degree holders - They were stagnating in the Highways Department without any prospect of career advancement - They accepted the option to be absorbed in the RD Department as Overseers, even though they possessed the degree qualification and having done so their claim for absorption as AE is without any legal or factual justification Service - Promotion - Appellants claimed that the promotion on the post of Assistant Executive Engineer ought to be made in the ratio of 1:1 as the direct recruits-Respondents are much younger in age - Appellants had already spent over 20 years in the Highways Department before their absorption in the RD Department, therefore, in case the promotions are to be based purely on the basis of seniority, the Appellants would never get a change to be promoted on the higher ranks - Held, prior to the absorption of the Appellants in the RD Department admittedly they had no chance of being promoted on the post of Assistant Executive Engineer, Executive Engineer or Superintending Engineer - It is only upon their absorption that they now enjoy a chance of being promoted on the higher posts - Fixation of the quota/ratio is the prerogative of the executive - It is not disputed that the ratio of 6:2:1 has been fixed in the service rules in exercise of the powers of the governor under proviso to Article 309 of the Constitution of India - In the absence of the Appellants placing on the record material to establish that fixation of such a ratio is patently arbitrary, the action of the Government couldnot be nullified - Fixation of quota on the basis of qualification is well accepted in service jurisprudence - Submissions of the Appellants that the ratio of 6:2:1 ought to be replaced with the ratio by 1:1 held to be devoid of merits Service - Exemption from rendering minimum period of service to claim promotion - Appellants sought exemption on the ground that since they possess the degree qualification they should be exempted from rendering five years service in the RD Department for being considered for further promotion - Held, Appellants had willingly given the option to be absorbed as Overseers - In case the submission made by the Appellants is accepted, it would mean that the Appellants were actually absorbed on the post of Assistant Engineer which would be factually incorrect - Under the rules, an Assistant Engineer can only be considered for promotion as Assistant Executive Engineer on completion of five years service in the RD Department - Therefore the submission of the Appellants that the services rendered by the Appellants in the Highways Department ought to be substituted for the service to be rendered in the RD Department held to be as not acceptable - In fact, the Appellants have already been given benefit of two years service in the Highways Department on the basis that they had actually been functioning in the RD Department since the relevant year but such concession would not create a legal right in favour of the Appellants to claim that the services rendered in the Highways Department ought to be treated as service rendered in the RD Department - Appeals were accordingly dismissed.

Brief Facts:

Since the facts involved in the controversy in all the appeals are common, we shall make a reference to the facts as narrated by the High Court. This shall be supplemented by any additions made by the parties in this Court.

The facts noticed by the High Court are that the members of the Tamil Nadu Rural Development Engineers' Association (hereinafter referred to as 'Appellants') were initially appointed as 'Overseers' by the then Highways and Rural Works Department and posted exclusively to various Panchayat Unions for executing all the Civil works/Rural works in the Panchayat Unions of Tamil Nadu. Since they were earlier under the administrative control of the erstwhile Highways and Rural Works Department, they had no proper avenues of promotion especially for the post of Assistant Engineer (for short 'AE') and many of them were languishing in the same post, i.e., as Overseers, for nearly two decades.

Held, while dismissing the appeal:

This Court, therefore, held that there is no reason why the Appellants on being absorbed in equivalent cadre in the transferred post should not be permitted to count their service in the parent department. The Appellants herein claimed the benefit of the previous service on the lower post of Overseer for determining the seniority on the higher post of Assistant Engineer. The aforesaid submission cannot be accepted for the simple reason that the Appellants had voluntarily accepted and given the option to be absorbed in the RD Department on the post of Overseer. No claim was made at that stage to be either absorbed or promoted as Assistant Engineer or to be given the benefit of the service already rendered by them in the Highways Department. Having considered the entire matter, we see no reason to differ with the view taken by the High Court. The appeals are accordingly dismissed.

CHAPTER NINETEEN

Chairman, Rushikulya Gramya Bank Vs. Bisawamber Patro and Ors., 2013

Hon'ble Judges/Coram:

Aftab Alam and Ranjana Prakash Desai, JJ.

Equivalent Citation: 2013(2)ESC357(SC), 2013(2)J.L.J.R.221, JT2013(8)SC436, 2013(2)PLJR309, 2013(5)SCALE251, (2013)4SCC376, (2013)2SCC(LS)291, [2013]4SCR239, 2013(3)SCT38(SC), 2013(2)SLJ144(SC), 2013(4)SLR773(SC), MANU/SC/0293/2013

Relevant sections:

Number of pages in original Judgment: 05

Case Note:

Service - Promotion - Criteria for assessment of merit - Challenge against thereto - Respondents, who were unsuccessful in getting promotions challenged select list of promoted candidates by filing writ Petitions before Orissa High Court - High Court held that prescription of benchmark of 60% marks in aggregate was in violation of promotion policy and Rules governing field - It accordingly directed Appellant-Bank to make fresh selection in accordance with Rules - Whether it was open to Management of Appellant Bank to lay down a benchmark besides criteria fixed by Rules for grant of promotion on seniority-cum-merit basis - Held, in taking view that prescription of minimum qualifying marks in aggregate was in contravention of promotion based on seniority-cum-merit, High Court relied upon decisions of present Court in State of Kerala v. N.M. Thomas, Bhagwandas Tiwari v. Dewas Shajapur Kshetriya Gramin Bank and B.V. Sivaiah v. K. Addanki Babu - Further in case of Rajendra Kumar Srivastava and Ors. v. Samyut Kshetriya Gramin Bank and Ors., present Court re-visited issue of fixing a high percentage as minimum qualifying marks for promotion on seniority-cum-merit basis - It examined all three decisions relied upon by High Court, namely, Bhagwandas Tiwari, B.V. Sivaiah and N.M. Thomas - In Rajendra Kumar Srivastava, Court observed and held that if criteria adopted for assessment of minimum necessary merit was bona fide and not unreasonable, it was not open to challenge, as being opposed to principle of seniority-cum-merit - Decision of High Court was contrary to view taken by present Court in Rajendra Kumar Srivastava - Therefore decision of High Court was accordingly, set aside - Select list prepared by Appellant-Bank was affirmed - Appeals allowed.

Brief Facts:

The Appellant - bank issued a circular No. 024/2004-05, dated June 23, 2004 notifying the vacancies inter alia in the seventeen posts of Middle Management Scale-II and eight posts of Junior Management Scale-I. The circular stated that the process of promotion shall be conducted as per the promotion rules of the Government of India. For promotion to the post of Middle Management Scale-II, the zone of consideration was four times the number of vacancies and for promotion to the post of Junior Management Scale - I, all eligible candidates were permitted to take the exam.

Held, while allowing the appeal:

The decision of the High Court, thus, appears to be clearly contrary to the view taken by this Court in Rajendra Kumar Srivastava.

The decision of the High Court is, accordingly, set aside. The writ petitions filed by the Respondents before the Orissa High Court are dismissed. The select list prepared by the Appellant-bank is affirmed. The appeals are allowed but with no order as to costs.

CHAPTER TWENTY

UNION OF INDIA (UOI) AND ORS. VS. HEMRAJ SINGH CHAUHAN AND ORS., 2010

Hon'ble Judges/Coram:

R.V. Raveendran and A.K. Ganguly, JJ.

Equivalent Citation: AIR2010SC1682, 2010(3)ALLMR(SC)942, (2010)3CALLT45(SC), (SCSuppl)2011(1)CHN112, 2010(2)ESC220(SC), [2010(125)FLR282], JT2010(3)SC240, 2010LabIC2174, 2010(3)SCALE272, (2010)4SCC290, (2010)1SCC(LS)1002, [2010]4SCR755, 2010(2)SCT421(SC), 2010(3)SLJ138(SC), 2010(3)SLR1(SC), (2010)2UPLBEC921, MANU/SC/0189/2010

Relevant sections: Rule 4(2) of Indian Administrative Service (Fixation of Cadre Strength) Regulations, 1956; Article 142 of Constitution of India

Number of pages in original Judgment: 08

Case Note:

Service - Promotion - Present appeal filed against order of promotion , granted in favour of Respondent - Rule 4(2) of Indian Administrative Service (Fixation of Cadre Strength) Regulations, 1956 - Held, statutory duty which is cast on State Government and Central Government to undertake cadre review exercise every five years is ordinarily mandatory subject to exceptions which may be justified in facts of a given case - Surely, lethargy, in-action, absence of sense of responsibility cannot fall within category of just exceptions - Neither Appellants nor State of U.P.

was justified in its action of not undertaking exercise within statutory time frame on any acceptable ground - Court can, especially having regard to its power under Article 142 of Constitution, give suitable directions in order to mitigate hardship and denial of legitimate rights of employees - Court is satisfied that in this case for delayed exercise of statutory function Government has not offered any plausible explanation - Respondents cannot be made in any way responsible for delay - Directions given by High Court cannot be said to be unreasonable - - Accordingly appeal is disposed of.

Brief Facts:

i. The respondents are members of the State Civil Service (S.C.S.) of the State of Uttar Pradesh and according to them completed eight years of service on 23.07.85 and 4.6.86 respectively. The contention of the respondents is that in terms of Regulation 5(3) of the Indian Administrative Service (Appointment by Promotion) Regulations, 1955, a member of the S.C.S., who has attained the age of 54 years on the 1st day of January of the year in which the Committee meets, shall be considered by the Committee, provided he was eligible for such consideration on the 1st day of the year or of any of the years immediately preceding the year in which such meeting is held, but could not be considered as no meeting of the Committee was held during such preceding year or years.

ii. Those regulations have been framed in exercise of power under Sub-rule 1 of Rule 8 of Indian Administrative Service Recruitment Rules, 1954 and in consultation with the State Government and the Union Public Service Commission.

iii. Regulation 5(1) of the said Regulation provides that such Committee shall ordinarily meet every year and prepare a list of such members of the S.C.S. as are held to be suitable for promotion to the service. The number of members of the said civil services to be included in this list shall be determined by the Central Government in consultation with the State Government concerned but shall not exceed the number of substantive vacancies in the year in which such meeting is held.

iv. It may be mentioned in this connection that as a result of bifurcation of the State of Uttar Pradesh as a result of creation of the State of Uttaranchal in terms of the State Reorganization Act, namely Uttar Pradesh State Reorganization Act, 2000 two notifications were issued on 21.10.2000. The first was issued under Section 3(1) of the All India Services Act, 1951 read with Section 72(2) and (3) of the Reorganization Act and Rule 4(2) of the Indian Administrative Service (Fixation of Cadre Strength) Regulations, 1956 (hereinafter referred to as the "Cadre Rule").

v. Thus, the Central Government constituted for the State of Uttaranchal an Indian Administrative Service Cadre with effect from 1.11.2000. On 21.10.2000 another notification was issued fixing the cadre strength of State of Uttar Pradesh thereby determining the number of senior posts in the State of Uttar Pradesh as 253.

vi. The case of the appellants is that the next cadre review for the State of Uttar Pradesh fell due on 30th April, 2003. To that effect a letter dated 23.1.2003 was written by the Additional Secretary in the Department of Personnel and Training, Ministry of Personnel, Public Grievances and Pensions, Government of India to the Chief Secretary, Government of Uttar Pradesh.

vii. The further case of the appellants is that several reminders were sent on 5th March, 3rd September, 17th September and 8th December, 2003 but unfortunately the Government of Uttar Pradesh did not respond. Then a further reminder was sent by the Government of India stating therein that four requests were made for the cadre review of the I.A.S. cadre of Uttar Pradesh but no response was received from the Government of Uttar Pradesh. In the said letter the Government of India wanted suitable direction from the concerned officials so that they can furnish the cadre review proposal by 28.2.04. Unfortunately, there was no response and thereafter subsequent reminders were also sent by the Government of India on 14th/17th June, 2004 and 8th October, 2004.

viii. Ultimately, a proposal was received from the Government of Uttar Pradesh only in the month of January 2005 and immediately preliminary meeting was fixed on 21st February, 2005. Thereafter, a cadre review meeting was held under the Chairmanship of the Cabinet Secretary on 20th April, 2005 and the Minutes duly signed by the Chief Secretary, Government of Uttar Pradesh were received by the appellants on 27th June, 2005. After approval was given to the said Minutes, notification was issued on 25th August, 2005 re- fixing the cadre strength in the State of Uttar Pradesh.

Held, while disposing off the petition:

Therefore, this Court accepts the arguments of the learned Counsel for the appellants that Rule 4(2) cannot be construed to have any retrospective operation and it will operate prospectively. But in the facts and circumstances of the case, the Court can, especially having regard to its power under Article 142 of the Constitution, give suitable directions in order to mitigate the hardship and denial of legitimate rights of the employees. The Court is satisfied that in this case for the delayed exercise of statutory function the Government has not offered any plausible explanation. The respondents cannot be made in any way responsible for the delay. In such a situation, as in the instant case, the directions given by the High Court cannot be said to be unreasonable. In any event this Court reiterates those very directions in exercise of its power under Article 142 of the Constitution of India subject to the only rider that in normal cases the provision of Rule 4(2) of the said Cadre Rules cannot be construed retrospectively.

CHAPTER TWENTY-ONE

State of Uttaranchal and Ors. Vs. Dinesh Kumar Sharma, 2006

Hon'ble Judges/Coram:

A.R. Lakshmanan and Altamas Kabir, JJ.

Equivalent Citation: 2007(3)ALT15(SC), [2007(114)FLR104], 2008(3)JKJ14[SC], 2007LabIC583, 2006(13)SCALE246, (2007)1SCC(LS)594, [2006]Supp()SCR1, 2007(1)SCT393(SC), 2007(2)SLR832(SC), (2007)2UPLBEC66, MANU/SC/5259/2006

Relevant sections: Rule 17 of U. P. Agriculture Group 'B' Service Rules, 1995

Number of pages in original Judgment: 08

Ratio Decidendi:

" A person cannot claim promotion from date of occurrence of vacancy but can only get promotion and seniority from time he has been substantially appointed as no retrospective effect can be given to order of appointment."

Case Note:

i. U. P. Agriculture Group 'B' Service Rules, 1995 - Rule 17--U. P. Government Servants Seniority Rules, 1991--Rule 8--Employment--Promotion -- Seniority -- Person appointed on promotion--To get seniority of year in which his/her appointment made--And not of any earlier year--Respondent cannot claim promotion from date of occurrence of vacancy in 1995-96--He can get promotion and seniority only from date he was substantively appointed in 1999--Seniority also to be counted against promotion/ appointment in cadre from date of issuance of order of substantive appointment in cadre, i.e. from 19.11.1999--No promotion or seniority can be granted retrospectively.

ii. U. P. Agriculture Group 'B' Service Rules, 1995--Rule 17--U. P. Government Servants Seniority Rules, 1991--Rule 8--Employment--Promotion--Respondent claiming promotion retrospectively in year of vacancy and also seniority accordingly--His representation rejected by Government by well-reasoned and speaking order--Respondent filing writ petition concealing this fact--Whether High Court justified in directing appellants to consider representation of respondent?--Held, "no"--It will amount to reconsideration of claim made by respondent.

Brief Facts:

i. On 25.10.1977, the respondent, Mr. Dinesh Kumar Sharma was appointed as Subordinate Agriculture Services Group-I on the post of Senior Chemical Assistant, Research (Chemistry) Branch through the Public Service Commission, U.P. Allahabad. Fifteen years service in Subordinate Agriculture Service Group-I is the eligibility criteria for being considered for next higher promotion. In the year 1992-93, respondent became eligible for the said promotion.

ii. On 31.03.1995, the Governor of Uttar Pradesh promulgated U.P. Agricultural Group II Service Rules 1995 providing for the selection, appointments, probation, seniority, promotion etc. Rule 21 states that the date of substantive appointment will be the basis of promotion. On 01.04.1996 and 01.05.1996, two class-II posts in the Hill sub cadre became vacant due to retirement of two officers. These appointments were to be made by Direct Recruitment as well as Promotion. Rule 17 states that, if in any year of recruitment appointments are made both by direct recruitment and promotion a combined select list be prepared by taking the names from the relevant list and "the first name in the list will be of the person appointed by promotion".

iii. On 19.11.1999, the Secretary to government of Uttar Pradesh of the Agriculture Department issued an order conveying that the respondent has been selected for subordinate Agriculture Service Class-I (Chemistry) in the substantive vacancy for the year 1997-98 in the scale of Rs. 8000-275-13500, after consultation with the State Public Service Commission.

iv. On 04.04.2001, the U.P Government Agriculture Department issued an order directing that those employees who were already members of the Hill Sub Cadre and posted at Uttaranchal have been finally allocated to Uttaranchal Government in which the name of the respondent was shown at serial No. 30. Thereafter on 17.07.2001 & 27.05.2002, the respondent made two representations to the Department contending that his seniority may be counted from the year 1995-96 with all the consequential benefits as the vacancies fell vacant in that year. Further on 12.06.2002, the respondent made another representation stating that his earlier two representations were not decided upon and that he should be promoted with effect from the date of occurrence of vacancy.

v. On 01.10.2002, the Government of Uttaranchal issued Office Memorandum conveying its decision of rejecting the claim made by the respondent.

Held,

In our opinion, the High Court should not have interfered with this finding of the Appellants and directed them to "consider" the representation of the respondent, which in effect will amount to the reconsideration of the claim made by the respondent. In the result, we allow the civil appeal filed in this Court by the Appellant, the State of Uttaranchal and set aside the judgment dated 29.03.2005 of the High Court of Uttaranchal. However, we are not ordering costs.

Videos & Tv Shows On Law & Exim

List of some important videos & TV shows on Law & EXIM by Adv. Jayprakash Somani on his YouTube Channel 'Jayprakash Somani EXIM & Legal'

Legal Videos: Hindi -English

1) SLP in Supreme Court / Special Leave Petitions in the Supreme Court of India

2) Transfer of Civil & Criminal Cases by the Supreme Court of India / Transfer of Matrimonial Cases

3) Appellate Jurisdiction of the Supreme Court of India

4) Jurisdictions of the Supreme Court of India

5) Public Interest Litigation in the Supreme Court of India / PIL in Supreme Court

6) Article 32 Writ Petitions in the Supreme Court of India

7) Bail Matters Top 10 Supreme Court Cases

8) FIR Quashing in High Court & Supreme Court

9) Bail & Anticipatory Bail Matters in Supreme Court

10) Insolvency & Bankruptcy Matters in the Supreme Court

11) Insolvency & Bankruptcy Code 2016 Part 1

12) Insolvency & Bankruptcy Code 2016 Part 2

13) Insolvency & Bankruptcy Code 2016 Part 3

14) Corporate Liquidation Process

15) Supreme Court Rules & Procedures Webinar of 2.5 hour on Zoom

16) RDDBFI Act, 1993 (Introduction)

17) The Indian Contact Act 1872

18) Negotiable Instruments Act (Introduction)

19) How to avoid matrimonial disputes& some more videos

20)SEBI Matters in the Supreme Court

21) Matrimonial Matters: Supreme Court's 20 Case Laws

22) Consumer Matters Supreme Court's 20 Case Laws

23) Service Matters Supreme Court's 20 Case Laws

24) How to Search Lawyer for Your Matter

25) Property Matters Supreme Court's 20 Case Laws

26) Bail Matters: Supreme Court's 20 Case Laws

27) Supreme Court / High Court Vacation Benches

28)69000 Teacher's Recruitment Matters of UP Government in the Supreme Court

29) Contempt of Court Matters in the Supreme Court

30) Advocate Act's Matters in the Supreme Court

31) Business Law Matters in the Supreme Court

32) Banking Matters in the Supreme Court

33) Labour Law Matters in the Supreme Court

34) Arbitration Matters in the Supreme Court

35) Careers in Law -Zoom Webinar by Adv. Jayprakash Somani

36) Civil Matters in the Supreme Court

37) Consumer Protection Act | Consumer Matters in the Supreme Court

38) Corporate Matters in the Supreme Court

39) Criminal Matters in the Supreme Court

40) Role of Respondent in the Supreme Court of India

41) Motor Vehicle Accident Matters in Supreme Court with case laws

42) Article 131 Original Suits in Supreme Court

43)PIL in Supreme Court/ Public Interest Litigations in the Supreme Court of India'

44)CAB Citizenship Amendment Bill is not Unconstitutional

45) Supreme Court of India Cases & Process – Marathi

46) Legal Services Export / Export of Legal Services

47) Transfer of Matrimonial Cases by the Supreme Court of India

48) Public Interest Litigation PIL

49) The Specific Relief Act (Introduction)

50) Corporate Insolvency Resolution Process CIRP

51)ABMM's Career 5 - Careers in Law

52) Transfer of cases by Supreme Court

53) Writ Petitions in High Court & Supreme Court of India

54) Supreme Court Jurisdictions - Appeals, SLP, Writ Petitions, Transfer, Original, Review, Curative

55)LEGAL INDIA TV Show: Cases Handled in Supreme Court

56) Corporate Liquidation Process

57) Legal Services Export / Export of Legal Services

EXIM Videos: Hindi -English

1) Yes, I can do Import Export Business Easily! 36 points excellent video in Hindi

2) Yes, I can do Import Export Business Easily! 36 points excellent video in English

3) Import Export Business – Hindi video

4) Import Export Business - English video

5) Export Import Marathi TV Interview

6) Scope for Commerce Students in International Business- TV Show

7) Scope for Management Student in International Business- TV Show

8) Scope for Engineering Students in International Business – TV Show

9) Women in International Business- TV Show

10) How to do Import Export Business Successfully!'

11) Where one can get full information on Import Export Business?

12) What to do import & export?

13) Import Export Workshop/ Training/Course/ Diploma

14) How to Start Import Export Business & How to grow it. Live Webinar

15) Success Stories & Failure Stories in Import & Export Business

16) For MSME Scope in Export & Import...

17) Exports In Agri. & Food Products – English & some more videos

18) Exports to Dubai, Aabudhabii. e. UAE

19) Jewelry Exports from India

20) How to attend EXIM workshop to become excellent Exporter

21) Import Export Best Training Course – Online & Offline

22) Agri Product Export

23) Scope for Woman in International Business

24) Management Graduates Scope in International Business

25) Pharma Product's Export

26) Best Import Export Course | Practical Training | Aaronica Global Exim

27) Import Export Business for Commerce Graduates

28) How Do I Get Export Orders? Finding International Buyers

29) What Is APEDA In Import Export Business?

30) Which Is The Best Product To Export From India?

31)EXIM Remark by Manoj Kumar Faridabad

32)EXIM Remarks by Mahesh Telangana

33) What Licenses I Need To Start Import/ Export?

34) How Can I Increase My Import Export Business?

35) Which Is Best B2B Website For Import/Export Business?

36) Export Import Management with Global Marketing

37) How to Start Export Import Business | 51 Points Video

38) Scope for Commerce & Other Graduates in International Business

39)BE A SUCCESSFUL EXPORTER FOR OUR NATION - Marathi video

40) Export of Textile , Cotton, Agri., Food, & other products & services

41) Exports from MP, CG, MH, GJ & CA in Fresh Fruits & Vegetables

42) Exports in Agri. & Food Products- Hindi

43) Start your Online/E-Commerce Business

44) How to Start Export Import Business & Grow it

45) Exports in Textile & Other Products

46) Start and grow EXIM business - Live English Webinar

47)'Import Export Business!' Why, Who, What &How can one do it easily!!

48) Live: Export of Product & Services During & After Lock Down Period

49) Frauds in Import Export Business

50) Import Export for Business Man

51) Import& Export for Women

51) Import& Export for Graduate & Post - Graduate Students

52) Agriculture Exports from India

53) Digital Marketing Setup - Marathi

54)2nd Secret of Successful Businessman

55) Digital Marketing Set up

56) Legal Services Export / Export of Legal Services

57) Export& Import with UAE

58) Service Exports / Exports by Service Providers

59) Import Export Workshop/ Training/Course/ Diploma

60) Exports& Imports with USA

61) Selection on Product for Export

62) Top Products Exported from India

63) What to do import & export?

64)ABMM Career 2 - 'Careers in Business & Industries

65) How to do Import Export Business Successfully!'

66)5 Secrets of Successful Businessman

67) Export from MP, Chhattisgarh &Vidarbha Nagpur

68)EXIM Hindi - Textile & Apparel Export

69)EXIM Hindi - Export Import Practical Training In Delhi, Kolkata, Mumbai and Pune

70) Import Export Business

71) Import Export Business Hindi

72) Import Export Business English video

73) Import Export Business Marathi

74) Women in International Business by Exim Guru Adv. Jayprakash Somani

75) Opportunities in Foreign Trade- Adv. Jayprakash Somani's special interview

List Of Adv. Jayprakash Somani's Books

1. Supreme Court of India's Leading Case Laws on 'Insolvency & Bankruptcy Code 2016'

2. Bail Matters – Supreme Court's Latest Leading Case Laws

3. Arbitration Matters- Supreme Court's Latest Leading Case Laws

4. Property Matters - Supreme Court's Latest Leading Case Laws

5. Matrimonial Matters- Supreme Court's Latest Leading Case Laws

6. Election Matters- Supreme Court's Latest Leading Case Laws

7.SEBI Matters- Supreme Court's Latest Leading Case Laws

8. Banking Matters- Supreme Court's Latest Leading Case Laws

9. Service Matters- Supreme Court's Latest Leading Case Laws

10. Contempt of Court Matters- Supreme Court's Latest Leading Case Laws

11. Consumer Protection Matters- Supreme Court's Latest Leading Case Laws

12. Corporate Law- Supreme Court's Latest Leading Case Laws

13. Supreme Court's AOR Exam- Leading Cases

14. Armed Force Tribunal - Supreme Court's Latest Leading Case Laws

15. Acquittal From 376 - Supreme Court's Latest Leading Case Laws

16. Negotiable instrument – Supreme Court's Latest Leading Case Laws

17. Contract Act- Supreme Court's Latest Leading Case Laws

18. Insider trading- Supreme Court's Latest Leading Case Laws

19. Foreign Exchange and Management Act- Supreme Court's Latest Leading Case Laws

20. Income Tax Act- Supreme Court's Latest Leading Case Laws

21. Company Law- Supreme Court's Latest Leading Case Laws

22. Competition & Monopoly Matters- Supreme Court's Latest Leading Case Laws

23. Compassionate Appointment- Service Matters- Supreme Court's Latest Leading Case Laws

24. Compulsory Retirement- Service Matters- Supreme Court's Latest Leading Case Laws

25. Voluntary Retirement- Service Matters- Supreme Court's Latest Leading Case Laws

26. Appointment by Seniority- Service Matter- Supreme Court's Latest Leading Case Laws

27. Promotion- Service Matter- Supreme Court's Latest Leading Case Laws

These Books are available online at

1. **Notion Press:** https://notionpress.com/author/jayprakash_somani
2. **Amazon:** https://www.amazon.in/s?k=jayprakash+somani
3. **Flipkart:** https://www.flipkart.com/search?q=Jayprakash%20Somani

Printed by Libri Plureos GmbH in Hamburg,
Germany